Coaches and Coaching Throughout the Ages

A JOURNEY THROUGH THE HISTORY OF CONVEYANCE TO THE MODERN DAY SPORT OF THE WEALTHY

BROUGHT TO YOU BY

The books created by Equine Heritage Institute are designed to preserve the history and majesty of the horse. Our goal is to find, understand, and pass on the valuable data about equine use and its influence on humanity. The Equine Heritage Institute is a not for profit 503(c) and 100% of all proceeds from the sale of books, services, and products support Equine Heritage Institute's mission.

To make a donation to EHI, please visit www.ehi-donations.com

SPECIAL THANKS TO OUR TEAM

Mary Chris Foxworthy, Research Writer

Mary Chris Foxworthy's grandfather owned one of the last creameries in the United States that still used horse-drawn milk wagons. This sparked Mary's life-long love affair with horses and passion for keeping their history alive. After graduating from college with a degree in Food Science and Communications, Mary Chris bought her very first horse with her very first paycheck. Since then, she has served on the board of various equine associations and held a judge's card in Carriage Driving. She is known for her work in the Gloria Austin Collection, and has published and presented numerous equine educational programs. She has written for several equine publications and won an award from American Horse Publications for one of her articles. Mary Chris is an active exhibitor in Carriage Driving and Dressage. Along with her husband, she enjoys spending time with their horses (three Morgans and a PRE), a bouncing Bearded Collie and two adult children.

Taylor Murray, Editor

Taylor Murray is a copy editor and creative writer who currently resides in Ocala, FL; also known as The Horse Capital of the World. Taylor is a professional in the Hospitality industry as an Event Planner, but her passion has always been writing. In 2015, she graduated from Florida Gulf Coast University with a bachelor's degree in Hospitality Management and a Minor in Creative Writing. After a few years of making sure hotel rooms were booked and parties were planned, she decided to pursue her passion in writing. Since then, she has written for business websites, completed her first collection of poetry, and hopes to one day publish a novel based on her life.

Gloria Austin's Collection of Books

www.GloriaAustin.com

ENJOY OUR OTHER BOOKS

- How a Horse Can Make You a Better Dancer
- The Brewster Story
- Carriage Lamps
- Gloria Austin's Carriage Collection
- A Glossary of Harness Parts
- Equine Elegance
- The Fire Horse
- Horse Basics 101
- The Unsung Heros of World War One
- The Horse, History, and Human Culture
- Horse Symbolism
- Horses of the Americas
- A Drive Through Time: Carriages, Horses, and History
- Speak Your Horse's Language
- Tea: Steeped in Tradition
- The Golden Carriage and the House of Hapsburg

Brought To You By The Equine Heritage Institute

Coaches and Coaching Throughout the Ages
By: Gloria Austin President of Equine Heritage Institute, Inc. (EHI)

First Publish Date 2019
Copyright © 2019 by Equine Heritage Institute, Inc.

Cover Art by Barbara Frake, Frake Fine Art

All rights reserved. No part of this publication may be reproduced, distributed, or transmitted in any form or by any means, including photocopying, recording, or other electronic or mechanical methods, without the prior written permission of the publisher, except in the case of brief quotations embodied in critical reviews and certain other noncommercial uses permitted by copyright law. For permission requests, write to the publisher, addressed "Attention: Permissions Coordinator," at the address below.

Gloria Austin Carriage Collection, LLC; Equine Heritage Institute, Inc.
3024 Marion County Road Weirsdale, FL 32195 Office: (352) 753-2826 Fax: (352) 753-6186

Ordering Information:
Quantity sales: Special discounts are available on quantity purchases by corporations, associations, and others. For details, contact the publisher at the address above.
Printed in the United States of America First Edition ISBN
978-1-7339860-3-8 - Print,   978-1-7339860-4-5 - Ebook

TABLE OF CONTENTS

Coaches - The Beginnings 8
    Roman Currus 9
    Hungarian Kotschwagen 10
    Early Coaches 11
A Great British Tradition 13
    Eras in British History 13
    Elizabethan Era 14
    Stuart Era 15
    Georgian Era 16
    Victorian Era 18
    Edwardian Era 20
The Evolution of Coach Construction 21
    Suspension Systems 22
    The Springs 24
    The Axle 26
    Brakes 28
    Some Innovations Did Not Catch On 29
Types of Coaches 30
    The Stagecoach 31
    The Mail Coach 38
    The Road Coach 49
    The Private Road Coach 54
    The Park Drag 57
    How to tell a Park Drag from a Road 64
Coaches in France 72
    Gala Coaches 77
America Gets Its Coaches 79
    The Horse Has to Get There First 80
    Roads and Carriages 82
    Westward Ho! 85
The Golden Age and the Gilded Age 88

Putting Together a Coach and Four 98
    Harnessing 98
    Coach Horses 100
    Driving a Four-in-Hand 106
    Attire 114
Coaching Today 117
    Clubs, Organizations, Associations and Museums 118
    Coaching Meets 122
    Shows 124
    Coaching with Gloria 126
Appendix 134
Timeline and Trivia 135
Sources 138

COACHES - THE BEGINNINGS

If you performed an internet search for "coaching" you would probably find a plethora of information about being a coach for various athletic endeavors or you might find information about life coaching. Perhaps you would even find information about bus schedules and high-end purses.

But…if the internet existed one hundred years ago, and you searched for "coaching", you would most likely learn all about driving a four-in-hand put to a coach.

Driving four horses, put to a coach, was an important method for carrying the mail and people from town to town in early England. Eventually, individuals began to drive private coaches. The Royals also began to drive in elaborate coaches as displays of their "royalty".

Today there are clubs, organizations, associations, museums, meets and shows to preserve the sport of coaching.

Our hope is that this book tells you everything the internet cannot about "coaching" and that you are inspired to even attend an event where you can see four-in-hands put to a coach!

The British established the tradition of private individuals driving four horses to a coach to replicate the four-in-hand style of the British coachmen who drove mail coaches and commercial road coaches over great distances and through the narrow streets of cities.

But people were driving "coaches" and multiple horses long before that!

Duke of Beaufort at Hyde Park, London.

ROMAN CURRUS

Roman currus, *or town chariot,* 100 B.C. *to* 400 A.D.

In Roman times, horses were driven abreast. The neck and girth harness, outfitted with a yoke atop the neck of the middle two horses, allowed the horse to pull, turn and stop a chariot without the aid of traces and pole straps.

Hungarian Kotschiwagen

It is often thought that the Hungarian Kotschiwagen, used around 1568, is the predecessor to the coach. It was developed in the Hungarian village of Kocs (pronounced "koch") which is on the road between Budapest and Vienna. In the 15th century, the village of Kocs made its living from building carts and transporting goods between Vienna and Budapest. Around this time, an unknown carriage maker in Kocs devised a larger, more comfortable carriage than any known at the time. It was called a Koczi szeter, a 'wagon of Kocs,' which was shortened to "kocsi."

It was driven by a professional driver, often standing, using his legs for softening the jar of the road surface since the vehicle had no springs or suspension, just as other early carriages. To soften the ride, passengers would also stand or sit on cushions that were filled with wool or other natural fibers. The breast collar and full collar harness, that were first used in China, had made its way to Eastern Europe by now.

Over the next century the kocsi became popular and was copied throughout Europe. The name became "kutsche" in German, "coche" in French, and "coach" in English. From the name of the English horse-drawn coach came all stagecoaches, motor coaches, and finally air coaches.

Early Coaches

A later incarnation of the Hungarian kosci positioned a seated coachman to drive the horses while the significant traveler was under cover. The vehicle underwent minor changes over time and eventually made its way to the west of Hungary. One variation was driven to three horses abreast which only requires two reins in the driver's hands.

English one-horse coach, 1616

The first coaches were fairly crude and little better than covered wagons, generally drawn by four horses. Without suspension, these coaches could only travel at around five miles an hour on the rutted tracks that served as roads at the time. During cold or wet weather, travel was often impossible. A writer of 1617 described the coaches as "covered wagons in which passengers are carried to and fro; but this kind of journeying is very tedious, so that only women and people of inferior condition travel in this sort." Most men rode astride a horse on a comfortable saddle.

A wood frame covered in leather protected passengers from the weather. The body was suspended from leather hung from an upright pillar protruding from the axles.

In 1564, Pope Pius IV was exhorting his cardinals and bishops to leave the new-fangled machines to women, and in 1588 Julius, Duke of Brunswick, found it necessary to issue an edict ordering his "vassals, servants, and kinsmen, without distinction, young and old, who have dared to give themselves up to indolence and to riding in coaches ... to take notice that when We order them to assemble, either altogether or in part, in Times of Turbulence, or to receive their Fiefs, or when on other occasions they visit Our Court, they shall not travel or appear in Coaches, but on their riding Horses."

English leather-covered coach 1696

Hackney coach about 1680

More stringent is the edict, preserved amongst the archives of the German county of Mark, in which the nobility was forbidden the use of coaches " under penalty of incurring the punishment of felony."

Rene de Laval was an extremely obese nobleman living In Paris. His only excuse for possessing a coach was his inability to ride a horse. (cited from: https://archive.org/stream/carriagescoaches00stra/carriagescoaches00stra_djvu.txt)

A GREAT BRITISH TRADITION

Coaching evolved out of necessity. First, it was to get the mail from town to town and then it was to get people from town to town. Eventually, individuals began to drive private coaches. The Royals also began to drive in elaborate coaches as displays of their "royalty". No longer was it considered taboo to ride in a coach; quite the contrary, it was a dispaly of wealth and status.

A good way to trace the evolution of coaching is to look at what was happening during the eras of British history.

Eras In British History

Tudor 1485-1603
      Elizabethan 1558-1603
Stuart 1603-1714
      Jacobean 1603-1625
      Caroline 1625-1649
      Interregnum 1649-1660
      Restoration 1660-1714
Georgian 1714-1837
      Regency 1811-1820
Victorian 1837-1901
Edwardian 1901-1910

The Gold Stage Coach commissioned by George III in 1760

Elizabethan Era   1558-1603

In Tudor times, transportation was slow and uncomfortable. Roads were just dirt tracks. Men were supposed to, by law, spend a number of days repairing the local roads but it is unlikely that did much good! In Tudor times, you would be lucky if you could travel thirty of forty miles in a day. It normally took a week to travel the one hundred ninety miles from London to Plymouth. However, rich people deliberately traveled slowly. They felt it was undignified to hurry and they took their time.

Queen Elizabeth's English coach, 1564

Queen Elizabeth I was Queen of England and Ireland from 1558 until 1603. This period of time was called the Elizabethan Era and was viewed as a time of prolonged peace. In 1564, she ordered a traveling carriage drawn by six great horses to journey from London to Warwick and it was reported, she was unable to sit down for weeks afterwards since these early carriages had no suspension to cushion the ride. Early coach bodies sat directly on the axles which has become known as a "dead axle". She persisted and often traveled in wagon trains of four hundred heavy horses pulling carriages and wagons full of provisions, servants and members of her court.

Queen Elizabeth's French Coach 1584

Queen Elizabeth's French Coach was a postilion driven carriage, where the driver rides the near horse (the ride horse) with reins in the left hand and the whip in the more dexterous right hand for directing the off horse (the hand horse) with a tap of the whip. This coach also has no suspension system.

Coaches and Coaching Throughout the Ages

Stuart Era 1603-1714

After the Elizabethan Era, craftsmanship and building systems improved and the coach began to evolve into a stately vehicle, suitable for the presentation of the wealthy and nobles.

London Hackney Coach 1625

In 1600 the royal posts were exclusively used to carry the king's correspondence. However, in 1635 to raise money, Charles I allowed members of the public to pay his messengers to carry letters. This was the start of the royal mail.

In 1663 the first Turnpike roads opened. You had to pay to use them and stagecoaches ran regularly between the major towns.

During this period the first North American British colonies were formed in the Western Hemisphere:
- Jamestown, Virginia in 1607
- Newfoundland in 1610
- Plymouth Colony in Massachusetts in 1620

This started the foundation for future British settlement and the eventual formation of both Canada and the United States of America.

This coach, produced in 1687, was considered to be a masterpiece. It came complete with gilded garlands of roses and was covered in crimson velvet.

Georgian Era 1714-1837

Transportation was greatly improved during the 18th century. Groups of rich men formed turnpike trusts. Acts of Parliament gave them the right to improve and maintain certain roads. Travelers had to pay tolls to use them. The first turnpikes were created as early as 1663 but they became far more common in the 18th century.

It was not uncommon for nobles to demonstrate their wealth by going out with six horses – the first two ridden postilion and the four trailing horses driven by a coachman from the box seat.

Kings and queens took pleasure in riding in the most elaborate of gilded carriages drawn by four, six and sometimes eight horses.

State Coach of King George III - 1761

Over time, these state coaches became ornate works of art, with carvings, glass windows, and intricate paintings on their panels. The bodies were hung on leather from uprights over the axle.

This Royal State Coach was built in Dublin in 1762 and used by every British monarch since George IV. It was gilded with painted panels by Giovanni Cipriani. There are three cherubs on the roof with four Tritons, one on each corner. The huge, heavy body is slung on Moroccan leather with gilded buckles. Measuring twenty-four feet long, twelve feet wide and weighing four tons (eight thousand pounds), it would have been pulled by eight horses. wearing red Moroccan harness. It had a removable coachman's seat so it could be driven postilion.

The Great Age of Coaching was from 1810 to 1830 when traffic reached frantic speeds of twelve miles per hour!

During this period King George III was deemed mentally unfit to rule, so his son, the Prince of Wales, ruled as his proxy and was king after his father's death in 1820. He was king for the next ten years until his own death. The George IV Phaeton (a type of carriage) was named after the Prince of Wales.

George IV driving a pony phaeton

The Regency Period saw great improvements in coach design and road construction, leading to greater speed and comfort for passengers. For example, in 1750, it took around two days to travel from Cambridge to London, but by 1820 the journey time had been slashed to under seven hours.

COACHES AND COACHING THROUGHOUT THE AGES

Victorian Era 1837-1901

During the 19th century life in Britain was transformed by the Industrial Revolution. Britain became the world's first urban society, and by 1851 more than half the population lived in towns. In 1829, English coachbuilder, George Shillibeer, launched London's first 'hail and ride' bus service and soon after, horse drawn omnibuses began running in London. In the 1860s and 1870s horse drawn trams began running in many towns.

Horse-drawn vehicles were one of the crucial sources of commuting during the Victorian Era. The aristocratic families and upper class families generally used a Barouche which was a four-wheel carriage with a fold-up hood. A Brougham was another mode of transportation which was used for daily traveling. The vehicle obtained its name after the man who designed it, Lord Brougham. Perhaps the most common cab was the Hansom cab named after its founder Mr. A.J. Hansom.

The wealthy still enjoyed the "splash and dash" in their own carriages pulled by matching horses tacked up in the best harness complete with crests. The carriages too were painted in the family colors and crests and the ladies especially delighted in this display of wealth. Coachmen's livery that matched the carriage interior, blankets, foot warmers, pillows, a clock, visiting list and cut glasses for drinks were "must haves".

Gentlemen's coaching gave driving its last hurrah in the 1890s. Wealthy gents took to driving large four and six horse coaches, normally driven by experienced coachmen in the past, and engaged in competitions amongst themselves.

Omnibus

Brougham

Barouche

Hansom cab

COACHES AND COACHING THROUGHOUT THE AGES

Edwardian Era 1901-1910

The Edwardian Era is one of the finest examples in modern history of an era truly in the crux of two very different worlds. The Edwardian Era is when we start to see more and more implementation of the standard inventions used in our modern world today. It became more common for homes of the middle to upper class to have electricity, phones, indoor plumbing and even a car.

London 1900

The Edwardian period was a decade marked by peace and prosperity at the height of the British Empire; indeed a "Gilded Age," both in England and America. Yet social relationships were strictly defined and interactions among and between the classes were governed by a series of complex and rigid rules.

The train had become commonplace and the poor were no longer reliant on what occupations they could find in their village and the rich were not ashamed to live conspicuously.

Carriages still filled the streets of London and were even more so in use outside of the city due to the poor roads. But it wasn't long before the cars began to take over.

London 1912

When the First World War broke out, marks of the lavish Edwardian period began to fade. With shocking speed, the old traditions became things of the past. Although interactions in England had been governed by rules of class and etiquette for centuries, the total social upheavals caused by war and industrialization wiped them away. As country houses in England fell into financial straits and were demolished or abandoned, the old, formal ways of life they represented were replaced by modern norms determined by a new and daring generation.

The times were changing. World War and the new king, King George V, would steer Britain into the Modern Era. Driving horses became a leisure activity rather than a necessity.

THE EVOLUTION OF COACH CONSTRUCTION

COACHES: REIGN OF QUEEN ANNE.

In the early days of coach and carriage construction, technology did not advance as rapidly as it does now. Advancements in suspensions, axles, springs, and brakes occurred over hundreds of years.

COACH OF QUEEN ELIZABETH'N LADIES.

Suspension Systems

Suspension systems began to make their way into carriage design as carriages evolved into fuller-bodied heavy coaches with passengers sitting on forward and backward facing seats in the interior.

These suspension systems were designed in part to smooth the ride in these horse-drawn vehicles, which were described as abysmal in the early days of carriages when roads and their maintenance were not developed.

Since metal work had not yet been developed into a leaf spring system, leather or chains suspended from upright struts supported the bodies of these types of coaches. The suspensions also kept the body of the carriage from shaking apart on rough roads or no roads.

The early suspension systems of leather straps and chains were used to prevent the body from resting on the axles.

The drivers often sat on a box, hence, the seat where the whip (driver) sits is called the "Box Seat". The box would carry tools in the event of a breakdown when traveling.

Suspension systems for bodies of coaches went from:
- Vertical uprights with chain or leather to
- S shaped uprights with body suspended on leather to
- **S or Whip Springs** with leather to
- **Cee Springs** with leather to
- A variety of other types including double grand suspensions which included two sets of springs and sometimes what is called a dummy spring (a curved piece of metal atop a leaf spring).

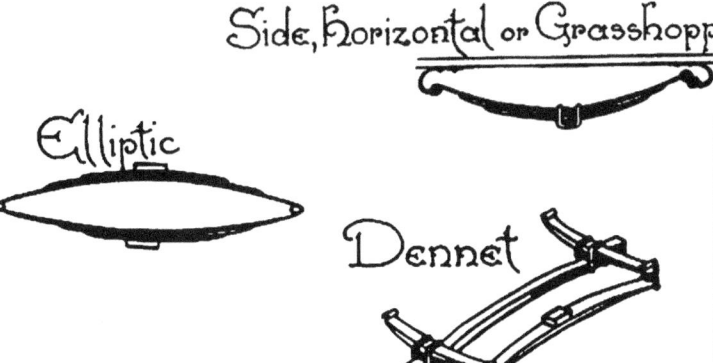

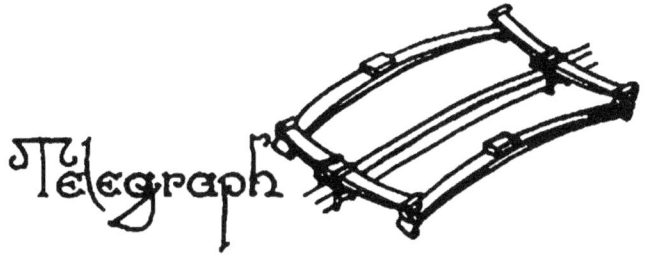

The culminating English Coach was positioned atop two sets of **Telegraph** or **Platform** springs, one set under the front boot and one under the rear boot.

These suspension systems will be noticeable on the various coaches shown throughout this book.

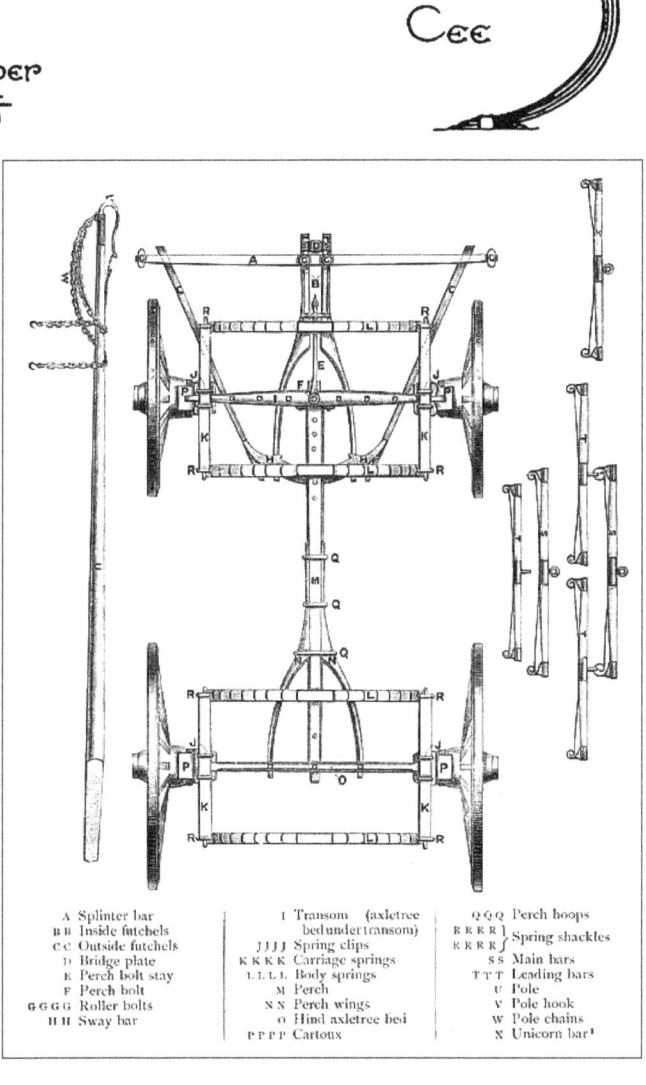

COACHES AND COACHING THROUGHOUT THE AGES

Springs

John Warde of Great Britain is credited with the suspension system used on English Mail Coaches. He found the coach box which rested on the front axle extremely uncomfortable and remedied this by placing a system of four sets of leaf springs between the front axle and the box seat. Warde persuaded the Manchester Telegraph to try his invention and they found the coachmen did not fall asleep and driving was easier.

The name of the coach, *Telegraph*, became forever associated with this type of platform spring. John Warde was also known as "the father of fox-hunting." His coaching craft was learned under the tutelage of Jack Bailey of The Prince of Wales coach.

The elliptical spring is made up of two sets of overlapping steel plates or leaves bolted together in an elliptical or semi-elliptical form. The elliptical spring made the ride on coaches and carriages much smoother and more stable.

Obadiah Elliott was a British inventor from Plaistow, Kent, who in 1804, patented the method of mounting coach bodies on elliptical springs attached directly to the axles, replacing the traditional heavy perch. He also invented the leaf spring by simply piling one steel plate on top of another by pinning them together. The leaf springs were shackled at each end to a carriage; it was the first ever leaf spring used on a vehicle. Four of these types of springs were used under the bodies of heavier coach type bodies. His invention was a major breakthrough in carriage design and it inspired a boom in the construction and sale of lightweight private carriages as well.

The impetus for the development of the light weight four-wheeled carriage in America occurred in 1807 when Captain Jonathan Mix perfected the elliptic spring (according to The American Date Book: A Hand-book of Reference Relating to the United States by W. E. Simonds). Captain Mix served in the Revolutionary War as a Captain in the Marines and was imprisoned in a Jersey Prison ship. After the War, he developed many different types of springs for carriages and is regarded as one of the fathers of that industry.

The Axle

The English Mail Axle was first adapted or applied to English mail-coaches that delivered the Royal Mail. These axles, although an old invention and possessing some disadvantages, are still considered superior on some accounts to the later Collinge Axle. They do not allow the escape of the oil from within the axle-box, and at the same time exclude the road dust, thereby preventing the wear of the axle.

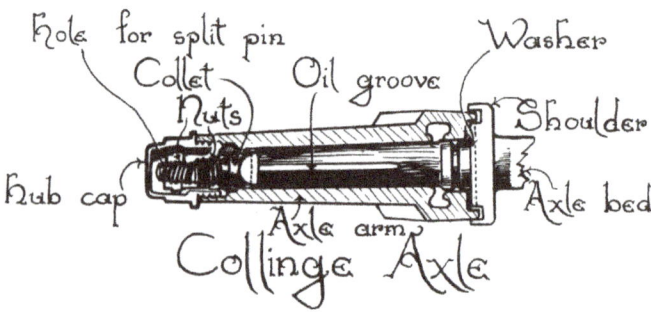

The disadvantages consist in the removing of three bolts, which run longitudinally through the hub, whenever it is necessary to detach the wheel from the axle. There is also a difficulty attending the application of washers to the axle and no provision is made for tightening up the hub to compensate for the wear of the washers.

They are not well adapted for light vehicles because of the extra weight of the metal plates and bolts. This type of axle generally appears on more substantial four-wheeled carriages and two-wheeled carts.

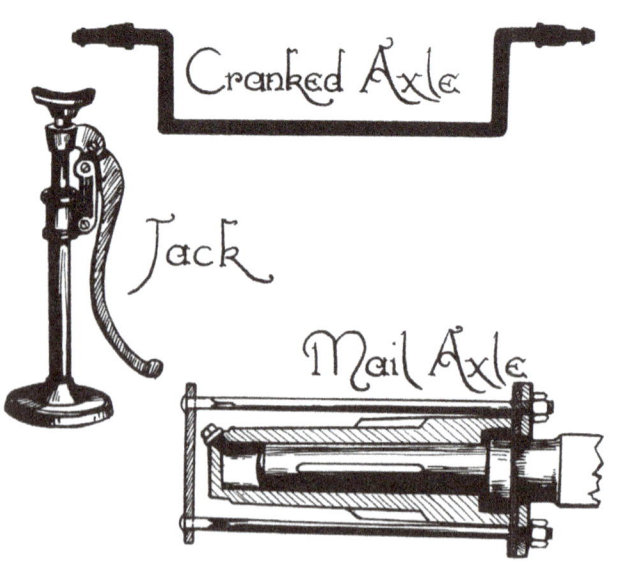

The Collinge axle was designed by John Collinge of Bridge Road, Lambeth in 1792. It was lighter in weight than the earlier British Mail Axle. Therefore, more popular with American manufacturers who were masters at making light weight carriages for their lighter weight horses.

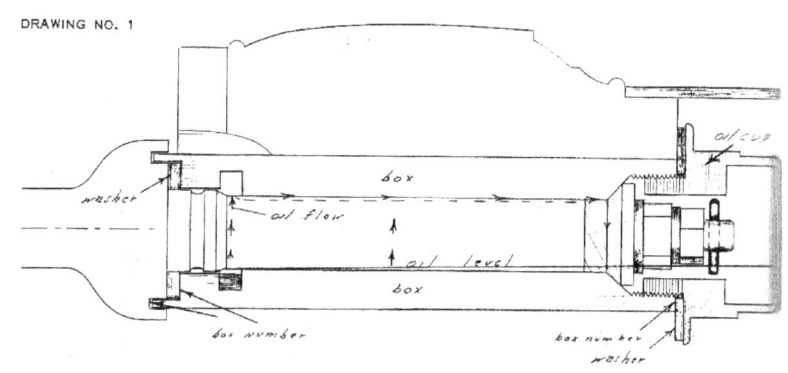

DRAWING NO. 1

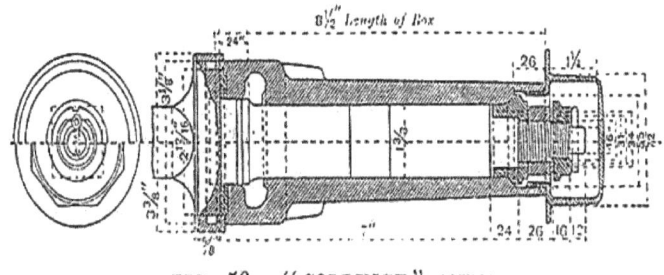

FIG. 56.—"COLLINGE" AXLE.

The axle box (bearing tube) revolves against a collar on the axle arm and has an oil reservoir at the inner end. It revolves against a collet at the outer end which is held in place by two nuts on opposing threads with a split pin through the outer nut. A brass axle cap is screwed into the outer end of the axle box. The cap is a second oil reservoir and is used to top up the oil. There was usually a groove machined along the top of the axle arm to assist the flow of oil from one reservoir to the other and also to catch any grit that may have entered. The axle arm and axle box were case-hardened. The oil is retained by a thick leather washer between the axle box and the collar and a thin one between the flange of the axle cap and the outer face of the stock or nave (wheelwrights never called it a hub). The axles and the axle box which turned on them were accurately ground together and their rotation pumped a supply of oil to the rubbing surfaces, so that a well-made Collinge axle could run for five thousand miles without any attention. Such axles were extensively used on horse drawn carriages and went on to mount the wheels of early motorcars a century later.

The Mail Axle is the older and heavier of the two types found on coaches. The Mail Axle is recognizable by the three bolts that extend through the hub with nuts on the inside where the nuts are visible.

Brakes

The horses are the real brakes of any carriage. All coaches have a pole end with rings mounted on a swivel crab so it can accommodate either pole chains or pole straps. The harness is adjusted so when the horses slow down, the carriage is held back through the use of the pole straps or pole chains attached to the base of the collar, or strap, attached to a yoke hanging on the front of the pole. The scrub brake, which moves against the rear tires, is operated by a lever of another mechanical system. A brake or skid shoe would be used on a steep hill and was put under one wheel of a heavy coach or wagon. Sleeve or band brakes are found on some carriages. On this type of brake, a band is mechanically tightened around a cylinder on the inside of the rear hub. Drum brakes are hydraulically assisted disk brakes that are found on modern carriages.

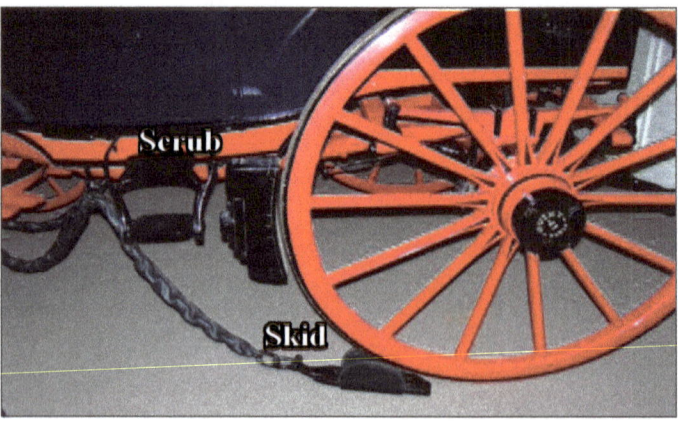

Some Innovations Did Not Catch On!

During the 18th century, varieties of carriages and innovations began to flood forth.

An extreme example would be this "automatic" carriage, designed to move with the aid of cogs and levers. The horns were operable and the dragon's head even shot water.

This carriage was actually used by Swedish Prince Gustavus.

George Pocock was an English school teacher and inventor, who taught at a school in Prospect Place, Bristol. Pocock had a huge interest in kites since his early childhood. As he grew up, he started experimenting with pulling loads using only kite power. He wanted to see if a kite could be used to pull a load on the ground. He tried various combinations and realized that a few large kites were capable of pulling a carriage with passengers.

His biggest invention came along in 1826, when he patented the design and called it a "Charvolant" buggy. His kite-drawn

carriage used two kites on a single line between fifteen hundred and eighteen hundred feet long. The vehicle was capable of drawing along a buggy carrying several passengers at an amazing speed for that time. Pocock documents the test rides in his book, "The Aeropleustic Art or Navigation in the Air by the use of Kites, or Buoyant Sails". The Charvolant managed to achieve a speed of twenty miles an hour over a long distance. On one of his journeys he passed the coach of the Duke of Gloucester. This was a serious breach of etiquette! Passing the coach of a duke was considered as a rude gesture. People were expected to stop and wait for him to pass them.

Most innovations did not catch on so, needless to say, people still preferred to use horses!

Coaches and Coaching Throughout the Ages

TYPES OF COACHES

Coaches developed first out of necessity. As times changed, clubs and organizations were formed and driving coaches became a sporting activity.

English Style Coach
    Stagecoach
    Mail Coach
    Road Coach
    Park Drag
    Private Road Coach

The French Style Diligence

Gala or Full-state Coach
    Berlin
    Dress Chariot

American Style Coach
    Concord Coach

The Stagecoach

Originating in England in the 13th century, the stagecoach, as we know it, first appeared on England's roads in the early 16th century.

A stagecoach is so called because it travels in segments or "stages" of ten to fifteen miles. At a stage stop, usually a coaching inn, horses would be changed; travelers would have a meal or a drink, or stay overnight, much like modern motels.

Jusserand states in "English Wayfaring Life in the Middle Ages" that coaches were introduced into England in 1564. He tells that the Coach was a strange looking monster that put horses and man into amazement. Some said it looked like a crab shell brought out of China and others imagined it looked like a pagan temple.

This replica was the type of coach in use during the reign of Elizabeth I (1558-1603). They had to be solidly constructed because of the terrible state of the roads at that time. Coaches like this were so heavy that, even when drawn by four horses, passengers only traveled a little faster than walking pace.

Claude Duval painting by William Powell Frith, 1860

In the 17th and 18th centuries, stagecoaches were often targeted by highwaymen such as Dick Turpin and Claude Duval. A highwayman was a robber who stole from travelers. This type of thief usually traveled and robbed by horse. Such criminals operated in Great Britain from the Elizabethan era until the early 19th century and were feared by stagecoach travelers. Claude Duval (1643 – 1670) was a French highwayman in England. He came from a family of decayed nobility and worked in the service of exiled royalists who returned to England under King Charles II. According to popular legend, he abhorred violence, showing courtesy to his victims and chivalry to their womenfolk, thus starting the myth of the romantic highwayman in novels. One famous story claims that he took only a part of his potential loot from a gentleman when his wife agreed to dance the "courante" with him on the wayside, a scene immortalized by William Powell Frith in his 1860 painting, "Claude Duval".

The first stagecoach route started in 1610 and ran from Edinburgh to Leith (approximately eight miles). By 1779 the stage coaches traveled between these towns one hundred fifty-six times a day!

Early coach travel was slow; in 1673, it took eight days to travel by coach from London to Exeter. However, the formation of a stage company in 1706 established a regular coach route between York and London and soon there were regular coach services on many other routes.

Coaching inns sprang up along these routes to service the coaches and their passengers. Many of these inns are still in existence today. They can be recognized by the archways which allowed the coaches to pass through into the stable yard behind the inn where horses were changed for fresh ones. In 1754, a company in Manchester began a new service called the "Flying Coach". The company claimed that the service would (barring accidents!) travel from Manchester to London in just four and a half days. A similar service began from Liverpool three years later, using coaches with the new steel spring suspension. These coaches reached the great speed of eight miles an hour and completed the journey to London in just three days. Speed of travel and comfort for passengers improved as roads and coach design improved. For example, in 1750 it took around two days to travel from Cambridge to London, but by 1820 the journey time had been slashed to under seven hours. This was the golden age of the stagecoach. Coaches now traveled at around twelve miles per hour, with four coaches per route, two going in each direction with two spare coaches in case of a breakdown.

The development of the railways in the 1830s had a huge impact on the stagecoach. Stage and mail coaches could not compete with the speed of the new railways. Soon the post was traveling by rail and by the mid 19th century, most coaches traveling to and from London had been withdrawn from service. (cited from: https://www.historic-uk.com/CultureUK/The-Stage-coach/)

Along the Great North Road, coaching inns provided refreshments, lodging and fresh horses for weary travelers.

The A1 highway now follows most of this route, only occasionally diverting from where the Great North Road cut through villages Leaving London, a coach's first stop would be Spaniard's Inn at the edge of Hampstead Heath. The famous highwayman, Dick Turpin used to stand atop the nearby hill spying out approaching coaches. After a successful "career" as a highwayman, he retired to run a stable stocked with stolen horses. It was a charge of horse theft, not highway robbery, that eventually sent him to the gallows.

COACHES AND COACHING THROUGHOUT THE AGES

It was long after the invention of coaches that a box seat was added for the driver and coachman. Before that, "The coachman joineth a horse, fixed to match a saddle horse to the coach tree, then he siteth upon the saddle, and when there were four horses he drove those which went before him, guiding them with a rein." (cited from: Annals of the Road by Captain Malet, p.12)

Sir Richard Gamon greatly contributed to the development of the box seat. Atop the front of an English style coach, a board was placed on the roof for passengers to sit upon when traveling. Named after him, this board, or the "Gammon Seat", eventually evolved into a more tolerable spot and was duplicated on the rear. However, before his advancements, people took stagecoaches from town to town and over long distances without any concern for safety. Parcels and mail shared the room on the coach along with passengers who took seating positions wherever available. The rocking motion of the coach caused several passengers to fall asleep and physically fall from the roof of the coach, hence the expression "to nod off" or "drop off." This risk to people's lives was championed by Sir Richard Gamon who introduced a private Member's Bill, which became law, restricting the number of outside passengers to be carried on a coach.

This law was opposed and mocked by many. People believed that limiting the number of passengers and cargo on their coach would recede their profits and was overall unnecessary. Although Gamon was only trying to help, others taunted him so much that a newspaper article was released about him and his law. In the article, the writers purposefully misspelled his name. This misspelling stuck and the "Gamon Seat" was forever spelled as the "Gammon Seat." (cited from: Stage-coach and Mail in Days of Yore by Charles George Harper)

The front Gamon seat faced forward and the rear Gamon seat faced backward. Passengers who rode on these seats were exposed to various weather conditions just like the driver and guard. Heavy wool coats (called "Great Coats") protected the outside driver and passengers from such harsh weather. Some coats had several capes layered over the shoulder area to further protect the passengers from the cold, rain, sleet, and snow. Even with the weather, these Gamon seats were often preferred to the prospect of sitting close to a smelly passenger on the inside of the coach.

The rider on the horse left room for more passengers and cargo

Sometimes where to sit was quite confusing - even for the royals.

King George III presented a state coach to the Emperor of China. The Chinese court had quite a discussion about who should sit where - they had never before seen a wheeled coach! The Emperor chose to sit on the hammer-cloth for his seat because he said it was nearest to the moon. The driver therefore sat inside and the reins were passed through the window. After a brief drive, with trumpets blaring and crowds cheering, the emperor descended in great pomp from his throne, with the severest resolution never to remount it. A public thanksgiving was ordered for his majesty's prosperous escape from a broken neck; and the state coach was dedicated as a votive offering to the god Fo, Fo (cited from: The English Mail-coach by Thomas De Quincey).

COACHES AND COACHING THROUGHOUT THE AGES

"Coaching was a ready-money business. The proprietors seldom owned the coaches but usually hired them from the builder at a rate of two pence to three pence per mile. The different proprietors horsed the coach each certain number of miles and, after all general expenses such as duty, tolls, wages and advertising had been paid, the balance was divided among the proprietors proportionally to the number of miles the coach was horsed. They had to meet the expense of providing the locomotive power (the horses) and here it was that knowledge and management must have been tested to the uttermost, for although the proprietors were all considered partners, yet each man provided his own horses and harness and any loss by death or otherwise in his stock fell upon himself solely and was not borne by the general body."(cited from: The Coaching Age by Stanley Harris)

Yard of the Swan with Two Necks - London 1831

The main function of the inn though was to provide fresh horses, though they provided other services as well, like hiring out post-chaises to allow travelers to continue on to outlying areas. In many ways, coaching inns were restaurant, hotel, travel agency, livery, repair shop and sometimes post office, all rolled into one. (cited from: englishhistoryauthors.blogspot.com)

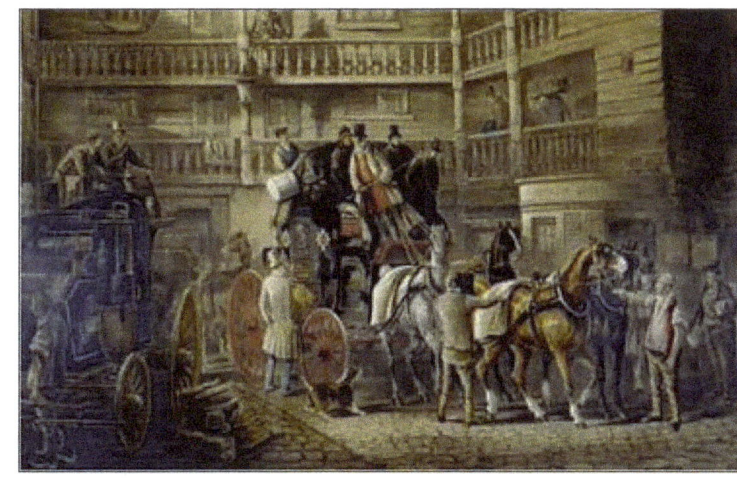

The Manchester Telegraph traveled the one hundred eighty-six miles from London to Manchester in eighteen hours and its celebrated coachman, Harry Douglas, was an enormous man who 'could gallop a coach without it swinging' and 'could drink as much as would scald a porker.'

The Manchester-Telegraph was built by England's greatest coachmaker John Vidler, with an improved lighter and stronger design, and devices for safety and comfort – including lowering the coach's center of gravity by bending the perch that connected the fore and hind axles. Springs for the coachman's box were henceforth in demand, and were known as 'Telegraph springs'. Previously coachman's boxes were forbidden springs in case the comfort induced sleep.

The principal proprietor of the Manchester Telegraph (whose name is on the door) was Edward Sherman who was one of the great coachmasters and stabled around seven hundred horses at the Bull and Mouth in St. Martin's-le-Grand. Like his great rival William Chaplin, Sherman had the vision to invest in railway stock and saved himself from ruin that most men of the road eventually suffered.

Royal Telegraph Manchester Day Coach by Robert Havell, published in 1834.

The Mail Coach

It was in England where the post rider truly began to serve all commoners in spite of the declared restrictive policy of the government as regards to their public use. In 1635, riders carrying the mail rode between "posts" where the postmaster would hand the new letters to the next rider. This system was less than perfect: the mail riders were often targeted by robbers and the delivery of the mail was slow.

A huge number of horses were involved in this operation as each stage was only about ten miles, after which a fresh horse was used. In most cases the horses were kept at inns or hostelries, and there were fixed routes of the service.

Merchants and farmers, constables and innkeepers, soldiers and sailors were using the post riders, attesting to the remarkable standard of literacy of the ordinary people.

At this time in England, it was a capital offense to steal a letter containing a bank-note or bill.

Due to time delays and dangers, it was decided to introduce Mail Coaches to transport letters and parcels in a faster, safer and more efficient way. Each Mail Coach had a guard. The guard (below) wore a scarlet coat because he was the representative of the King or Queen. Note the pouch that carried the time piece, key to the boot and the weigh bill listing the parcels and mail on board. He also was in charge of security so he carried a blunderbuss (a short-barreled large-bored gun with a flared muzzle, used at short range) in case of highway robbery. His other function was to announce the presence of the mail with a coaching horn. The most common call was "Clear the Road" for the Royal Mail.

A Royal Mail Coach came into use in 1784. It was designed to make the mail-carrying safer than having riding post-boys carry the mail.

By 1797, there were forty-two coach routes throughout the country, linking most major cities and carrying both stagecoaches and mail coaches.

England is indebted to John Palmer for the institution of the mail coach system. As Mr. Palmer noted, "The mails used to be generally entrusted to some idle boy without character, who was mounted on a worn-out hack, and who was far from being able to defend himself or to escape from a robber and was more likely to be in league with him." Sometimes tradesmen sent letters by stage coach on account of the frequent robberies of letters sent by the post-boys. "Why, therefore," said Mr. Palmer "should not the stage coach, well protected by armed guards, under certain conditions to be specified, carry the mail bags?" A stage-coach between London and Bath did the journey in one day whereas a letter took three. Palmer presented a paper called "A Plan for the Reform and Improvement of the General Post Office" to Mr. Pitt, the Chancellor of the Exchequer (later Prime Minister), who saw the merits of Palmer's idea. Palmer proposed that, instead of leaving London at all hours of the night, all the coaches for the different roads should start from the General Post Office at the same time. There was much opposition to his plan but, despite that, the first Mail Coach on Palmer's system began running on August 8, 1784. The same day Mr. Palmer was installed at the Post Office under the title of Controller General. The mails under the new system traveled safely throughout the country and, for many years after their introduction, not a single attempt was made in England to rob them.

At the time though, roads were either dirt paths susceptible to rain and mud, or very expensive stone roads that frequently broke down. John Loudon McAdam was a Scottish engineer who was convinced that massive stone slabs would not be needed to carry the weight of the mail coaches and other carriages as long as the road was kept dry. McAdam came up with the idea of raising roadbeds to ensure adequate drainage. He then designed these roadbeds using broken stones laid in symmetrical, tight patterns and covered with small stones to create a hard surface. McAdam discovered that the best stone or gravel for road surfacing had to be broken or crushed, and then graded to a constant size of chippings. McAdam's design, called "MacAdam roads" and then simply "macadam roads," represented a revolutionary advancement in road construction at the time. By making roads both significantly cheaper and more durable, McAdam triggered an explosion in road building with roads sprawling out across the countryside.

Eventually, it was decided that all the mail coaches should be both built and furnished on one plan. For many years, the contract for building and repairing a sufficient number of them was given to Mr. John Vidler, who had suggested many improvements in their construction. Although the post-office authorized and arranged for the building of the coaches, the mail contractors were required to pay for them. The official control of the coach and mail-guards was the duty of the Superintendent of Mail Coaches, whose head-quarters were at the General Post Office.

John Palmer was responsible for many improvements such as building lighter coaches and improving their punctuality. Coaches were timed to the minute; horses waiting for the changes; stages rarely exceeded eight miles with one set of horses; twenty minutes was allowed for dinners at the inns along the way.

Once passenger seating was available and a guard insuring punctuality, the mail coach was the desired form of travel since there was to be no delay of the Royal Mail. It was said, "You know the time by the mail." (The passing of the Mail Coach.)

John Palmer's First Mail Coach by Maile (1922–2017)

Mail Coaches carried the Royal Seal on the lower door panel and an identifying number was painted on its side along with the destination town. The front seat, on wooden risers, was for the driver and a single passenger. It was called a "box seat" since the early coaches had a simple box on which the driver sat. The guard wore a uniform with a scarlet jacket and had a blunderbuss in an accessible box at the rear of the body. Six passengers rode inside. Some passengers rode on the roof on top of baggage and parcels which were secured with straps.

Mail Coaches eventually took passengers on a front Gamon seat but never had a back Gamon seat. The absence of a rear-facing roof seat prevented passengers from blocking the entrance to the rear boot which opened from the top near the guard's feet. Sturdy Mail Axles with hubs, secured with plates on both sides and three bolts passing from plate to plate, were commonplace on these vehicles. This was developed so the wheel could not come off the axle.

Hull-London Royal Mail Meeting a Traveling Chariot on the Road

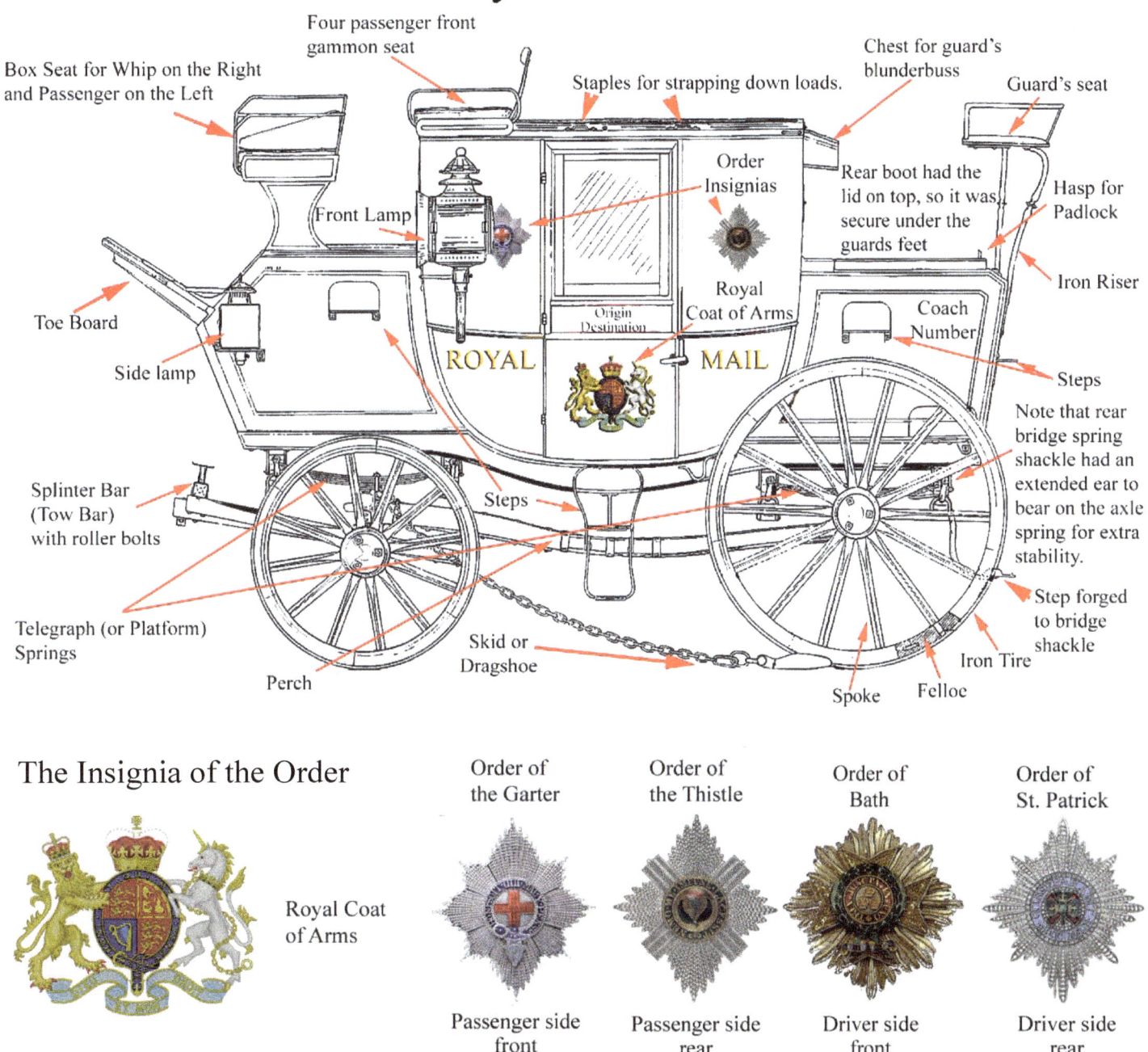

In the coaching heyday, 700 Mail Coaches covered 1,200 miles every night. A further 3,300 stagecoaches also ran daily covering many more miles. 150,000 horses were used, most of them driving 6-7 miles out and back home. The average cost of a horse was 25 pounds, and a set of harness cost 14 guineas (14 pounds, 14 shillings). The coaching business even provided jobs for 30,000 men!

Birmingham-London Royal Mail at a Country Post Office

Stops to collect mail were short and sometimes there would be no stops at all with the guard throwing the mail off the coach and snatching the new deliveries from the postmaster. At times the mail was suspended on a post.

The mail coach was faster than the stagecoach as it only stopped for delivery of mail and generally not for the comfort of the passengers.

Exeter-London Royal Mail Passing William Downe's Exeter Waggon

The coach was drawn by four horses and had seating for four passengers inside. Further passengers were later allowed to sit outside with the driver, but never on the back seat with the guard.

Royal Mail at Daybreak

COACHES AND COACHING THROUGHOUT THE AGES

The mail was held in a box to the rear, where a Royal Mail post office guard sat or stood.

The Shrewsbury Wonder Meeting the Holyhead-London Royal Mail

The coaches averaged 7 to 8 mph (11–13 km/h) in the summer and about 5 mph (8 km/h) in the winter, but by the time of Queen Victoria, the roads had improved enough to allow speeds of up to 10 mph (16 km/h). Fresh horses were supplied every 10 to 15 miles (16–24 km).

Hull-London Royal Mail with Extra Passengers

The Rural Post Office by John Sturgess

Making Way For The Mail by John Sturgess

Alfred F. De Prades (1844-1883) Summer Royal Mail Coach

Mail Coach in a Thunder Storm on New Market

Mail Coaches were slowly phased out during the 1840s and 1850s even though gentleman drivers continued to use the roadways. The Mail Coach was gradually replaced by trains as the railway network expanded.

The Road Coach

The demand for seating and parcel delivery warranted a coach for commercial fares for traveling. Each of these coaches sported a name. This one is called "Sir Walter Scott" after the famous romantic author. These coaches followed a defined route from town to town just as the Mail Coaches. Stops were generally eight to twelve miles apart, depending on terrain. Sometimes an extra horse would be positioned at the bottom of a hill to add extra horsepower for the assent. This pulling horse was ridden and returned to the stable to assist the next passing coach.

The horses pulling the Road Coach could be of various or mixed colors. They had to be strong and sturdy to hold up for commercial use.

These Road Coaches had to be of bright colors with its stops and destinations painted on the body to draw attention and encourage people to travel by coach on land rather than waterways.

Unlike the Mail Coach with no brakes or ladder, this Road Coach had two sets of scrub brakes plus a brake shoe, since it carried the additional weight of many passengers and parcels. The ladder is needed now to aid passengers atop the coach.

COACHES AND COACHING THROUGHOUT THE AGES

A public coach carried fare paying passengers over a regularly scheduled route.

A professional guard in scarlet livery with access to a blunderbuss and horn traveled on the rear seat facing forward. He also carried the key to the boot and weigh bill in a pouch strapped cross his body.

These coaches were built heaver than a Park Drag because they had to take the wear and tear of long travel over roads that might not have been in the best repair.

The Gamon seats had fixed backs that did not fold away. The rear seat was wide enough for the guard and three other passengers.

The guard was seated on the left or near side of the coach where the stick basket made of leather held walking sticks, umbrellas and the post horn.

Iron rails running on the outside roof seat rail were laced with leather to prevent the luggage on the roof from falling off the top of the coach.

Road Coach

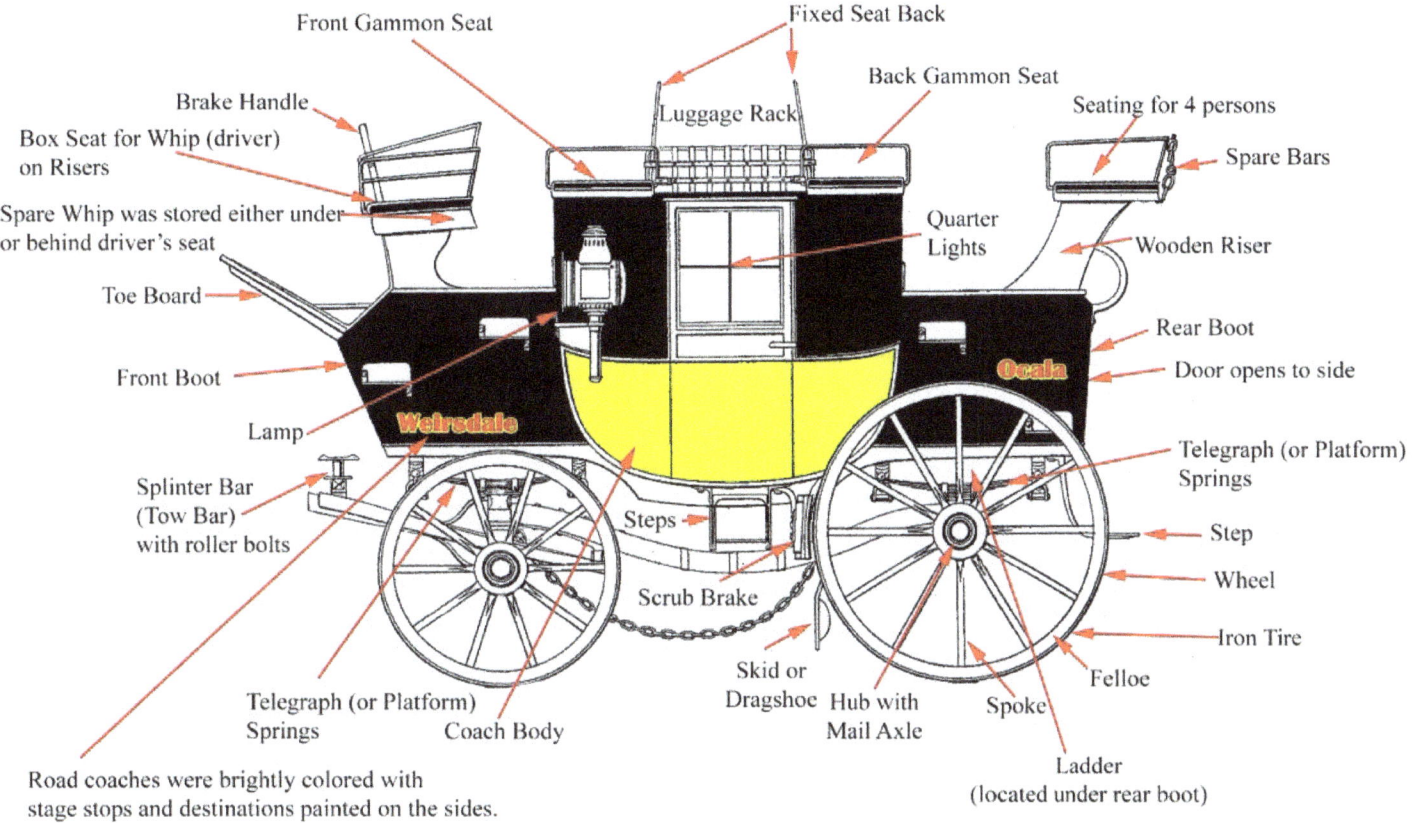

Coaches and Coaching Throughout the Ages

The Road Coach harness is simple and single stitched for practical and economical purposes. The collars are brown and went with each horse and often one for summer and one for winter to fit the horse as its weight might vary from season to season. The hame anchor had a ring for attachment to the tug and the horses each carried a ring on the kidney link as they may have switched from leader to wheeler where the ring accommodated the pole chain.

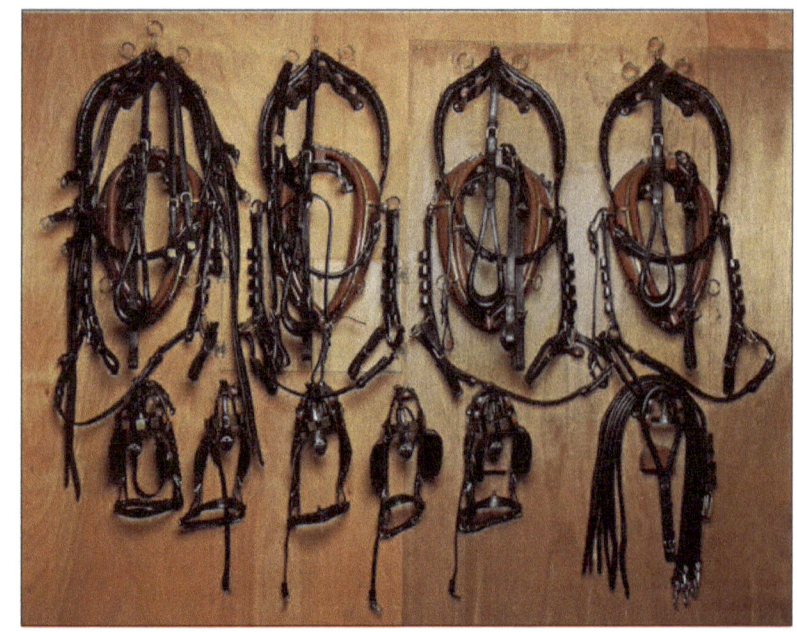

The bridles carried a "hit or miss" brow band and did not carry a decorative fob suspended from the poll piece that would have been seen at the front of the horse's face on a Park Drag harness. The bits would have varied according to the needs of the coachman for control and the pleasure of the horse to respond.

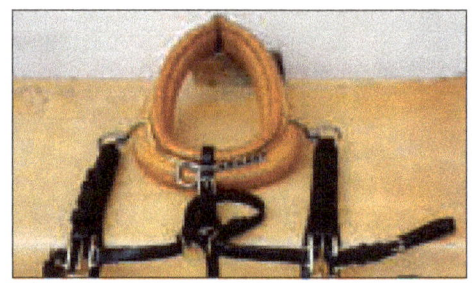

The Cock Horse was outfitted with a saddle and was stationed at the bottom of the hill to provide extra horsepower for the assent. A very sturdy rope was carried so the cock horse could easily be attached to the coach, running between the two pairs along the pole, to assist on steep inclines.

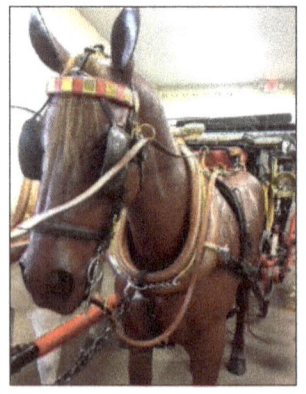

Coaches and Coaching Throughout the Ages

At one of the Austin Horse Park Carriage and Horse Festivals, Gloria Austin presented four Kladrubers to a Lawton Road Coach. The coach is trailed by a Cock Horse which traditionally would have been positioned at the bottom of a hill to provide extra horsepower for the assent. The cock horse would have been hitched in front of the four and attached to the coach with a rope feeding between the two pairs of horses and attached to the tow bar (or splinter bar).

The Private Road Coach

Private Road Coaches are coaches which combine elements of both the Park Drag and the Road Coach. There are well over two hundred variations of these coaches with these combined characteristics. The coach at the right is a good example. It is painted like a Park Drag. The rear seat accommodates two grooms like a Park Drag but has wooden risers like a Road Coach. The Gamon seats fold down like a Park Drag, but it carries a luggage rack between the two seat backs, like a Road Coach.

Private Road Coach by Guiet of Paris

These coaches were used for travel between town house and country estate or journeys of longer distance for touring rather than to the park or a race meet on a Sunday afternoon.

They were owned by wealthy people for private travel with invited guests on board. They could be driven by the owner or a coachman.

Private Road Coach
- Driven by owner
- For chosen tour or traveling
- No fare paying passengers
- A designated route
- Normally not given a name
- Usually carrying two grooms in informal livery
- Guard not necessary

Coaches and Coaching Throughout the Ages

English style Private Road Coach

This Private Road Coach has more features of a Park Drag than a Road Coach. The rear groom's seat accommodates two liveried grooms and is on iron risers. It has a single light (window glass) and is painted in somber colors with matching dark upholstery.

There are a few characteristics of a Road Coach. The rear boot opens to the side and is set up for carrying supplies for road travel rather than presentation of a picnic. Traveling coaches would have been set up this way so that attendants would have easy access to the tools needed for care of the horses and repairs that might be needed for long distance travel.

Halters and lead lines, water buckets, an oil can, wrenches, a spares bit, farrier tools, a hand-held lamp, an extra kidney link and hame strap (parts to the harness collar) would have been placed or hung in specific designated places in this rear boot.

This private Road Coach carries the number 23869. The hub caps and plates on the interior of doors, read Brewster & Co. New York. This coach was built in 1902 for Henry Pratt McKean of Philadelphia, President of the Philadelphia Four-in-hand Club and member of the New York Coaching Club. This coach weighs two thousand eight hundred seventy-five pounds.

The coach body is lined with an exceptional caning making it easy to see inside where rain wear and lap robes would be stored.

From the original order in the Brewster records, it was discovered that the coach has hinged lazy backs on the Gamon seats. A hat rack and ten coat hooks adorn the interior. There is a shutter mirror on the near side door. Aprons and quarter sheets for the horses were ordered in burgundy to match the coach's upholstery.

After Mr. McKean's death in 1922, the coach was purchased by MGM Studios and appeared in "A Tale of Two Cities" with Ronald Coleman and a 1935 production of "A Christmas Carol". This coach was originally restored by Joel Brown and is, as of this writing, owned by Wayne and Frances Baker.

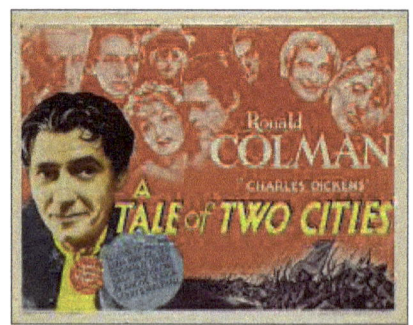

COACHES AND COACHING THROUGHOUT THE AGES

The Park Drag

This style of coach was used for private driving by wealthy men and women. It was often seen taken to the park or the hunt races on a sunny weekend.

It was generally of somber colors with only a discrete family crest on the crest panel just below the "light," which is what they called a glass window in a carriage. One might think the "light" was the lamp. The coach can be presented with either the light exposed or with shutters (a solid wood panel to match the colors of the coach).

The horses of this coach are to be perfectly matched in color and way of going or one could have an attractive cross team (light and dark horse at a diagonal in a checker board pattern).

The Park Drag gave birth to the Tailgate Picnic since the rear boot door folded downward to form a platform for serving food. The picnic supplies were carried in the rear boot, the body of the coach and in the Imperial, a box between the front and rear Gamon seats.

The British were particularly adept at keeping their coaches to particular standardized characteristics. When private coaching became popular, many Road Coaches were converted to Park Drags.

This coach is by Shanks of London, one of Great Britain's most famous manufacturers. It has all of the characteristics of a pure Park Drag

Park Drag

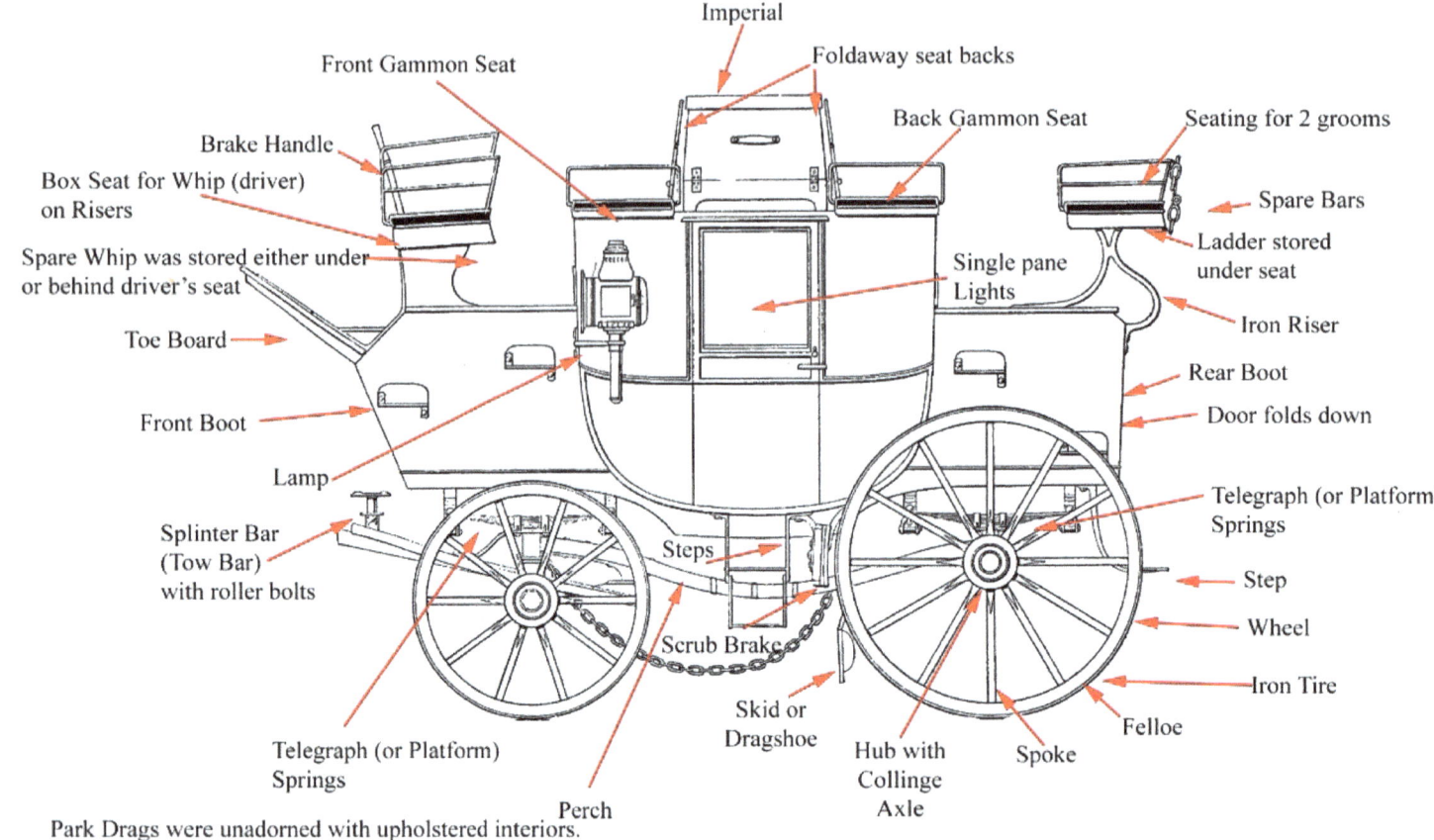

Park Drags were unadorned with upholstered interiors.

Park Drags are typically lighter in weight than Mail and Road Coaches. Park Drags have ten spokes in front and twelve spokes behind, whereas the heavier Road Coaches have twelve spokes in front and fourteen spokes behind. The reason many English Park Drags have twelve and fourteen spokes is because they were Road Coaches converted to Park Drags. The Gamon seats on this coach sit only three instead of four persons each. This coach holds a wooden ladder under the rear seat which is unlike most park drags that have iron ladders in this position.

The red ribbon awards are for first place in Canada

The term Grandstand comes from sitting atop a coach to observe horse races or polo matches of a bygone era. The horses would be unhitched and people would sit in the high position to see the activities of the day. Food and beverages might be served from the refreshments carried in the rear boot or in a hot food chest placed on the floor between the two interior seats.

COACHES AND COACHING THROUGHOUT THE AGES

The imperial could be of wood, leather or wicker and carried on the rooftop of a park drag between the Gamon seats.

It carried provisions or equipment for a picnic in the park. Sometimes there would be a set of light weight wooden folding chairs and a table.

A basket for walking sticks (which were the fashion of the day) and umbrellas would be carried on the near side of the park drag. A similar basket made usually of leather would be carried on a road coach.

Some Coaches were equipped with a canopy for protection from the sun or rain.

The inside seats were never used for passengers, but sometimes servants would ride inside a coach to serve food and beverages at the picnic stop.

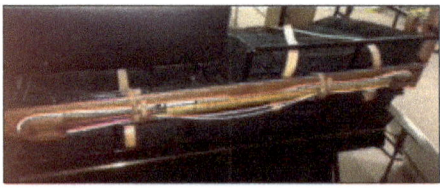

A spare whip is carried on the front (most usually) or back of the box seat (driver's seat) so it is readily available if the driver should break his or her whip along the way.

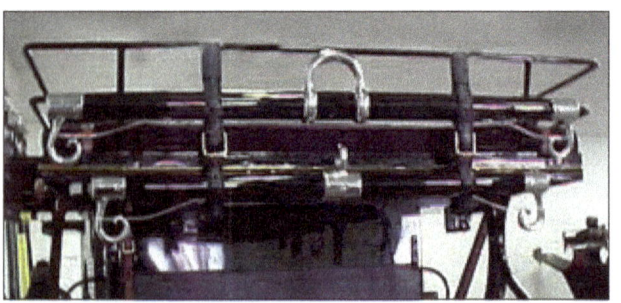

Spare bars were carried on most types of coaches and were positioned on the back of the rear groom's seat so they are readily available for the grooms or coachman to change a lead bar if broken. The main bar is on top since it is least apt to break. The side bar is carried on the bottom. All screw heads should be visible.

Coaching bars have a U shaped bracket called a shackle on the main bar that is positioned over the shepherd's hook at the end of the pole.

If the main bar is outfitted with a round ring eye, it is for a lesser carriage without a perch. The bottom picture shows a set of bars for a lesser carriage.

Coaching bars

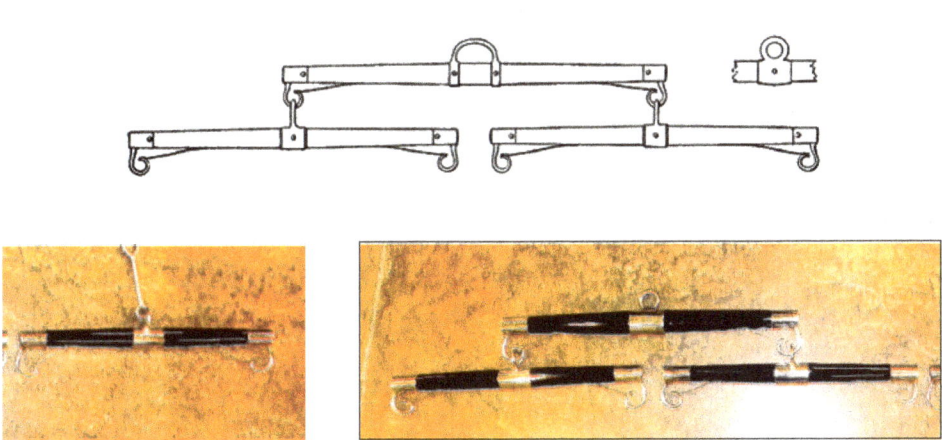

A unicorn hitch is made up of a pair of horses with a lead horse in the middle; in this case a unicorn bar is used. It is outfitted with an extension to compensate for the missing main bar when driving just one horse in front of the pair attached to the carriage.

Drivers, or whips as they are called, could carry a unicorn bar and a set of tandem reins in the event one of the four is injured or lame.

Coaching pole with Shephers's hook

COACHES AND COACHING THROUGHOUT THE AGES

A Drag with a team of well-matched strawberry roans

Wealthy men always wanted to replicate the skill of the British coachman and took to driving four horses put to Park Drags. It was a way to show off their wealth and skill as well as social status.

An afternoon jaunt in a Drag

Mail Coaches were slowly phased out during the 1840's and 1850's even though gentleman drivers continued to use the roadways. The Mail Coach was gradually replaced by trains as the railway network expanded.

Brewster (American) Park Drag

Holland & Holland (English) Park Drag

How To Tell A Park Drag From A Road Coach?

The actual function of the Park Drag versus the Road Coach determines many of the features, the harness used and even the horses used.

SEATS

There is no back on the box seat where the whip or driver sits on the Road Coach. This allows the whip to lean back when necessary to control the horses. The passenger's seat beside the whip can have a back that is sometimes made removable.

Gammon seat backs are hinged on a Park Drag and should be folded down when there are no passengers occupying the seat. They should always be padded.

REAR SEAT RISERS

Park Drag: iron risers
Seats Two

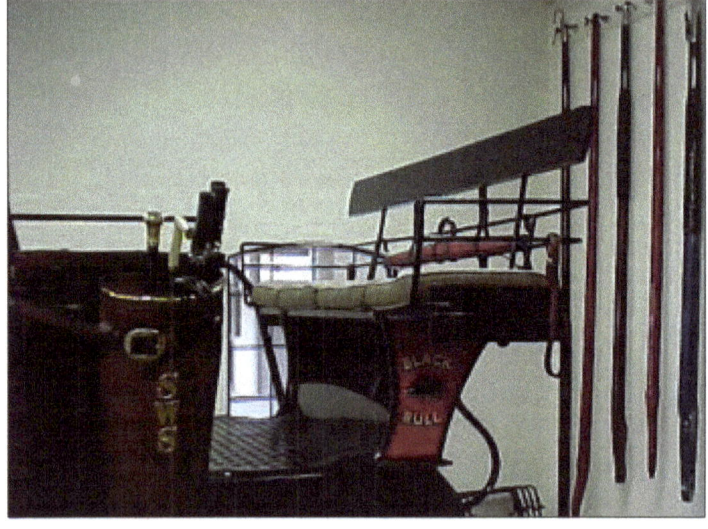

Road Coach: wooden riser
Seats Four

TYPE AND LOCATION OF LADDER

Park Drag: under groom's seat

Road Coach: under rear boot

TAILGATE DOOR

Park Drag:
opens downward for table

Road Coach:
opens to the side for access to appointments

TAILGATE CONTENTS

Park Drag: cellarettes for food and libations

Road Coach: appointments

LIGHTS (WINDOWS WITH GLASS)

Park Drag: full pane of glass

Road Coach: quarter lights

DOOR PANELS

Park Drag: simple monogram or crest

Road Coach: name of coach destination and pick-up stations

BETWEEN GAMON SEATS

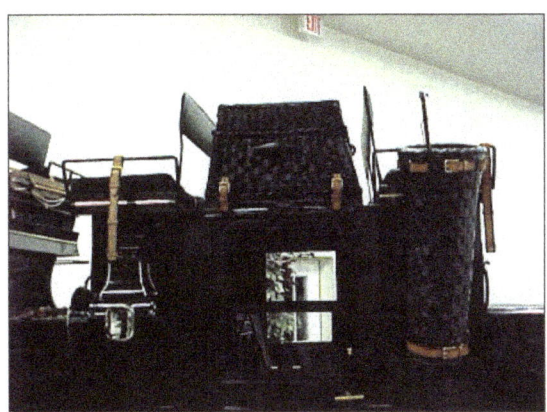

Park Drag: wicker imperial to carry food and libations

Road Coach: straps to contain parcels and cases

INTERIORS

Park Drag

- Leather, silk, or wool broadcloth trimmed in coach lace
- Door pockets for small items
- Leather hat rack on ceiling

Road Coach

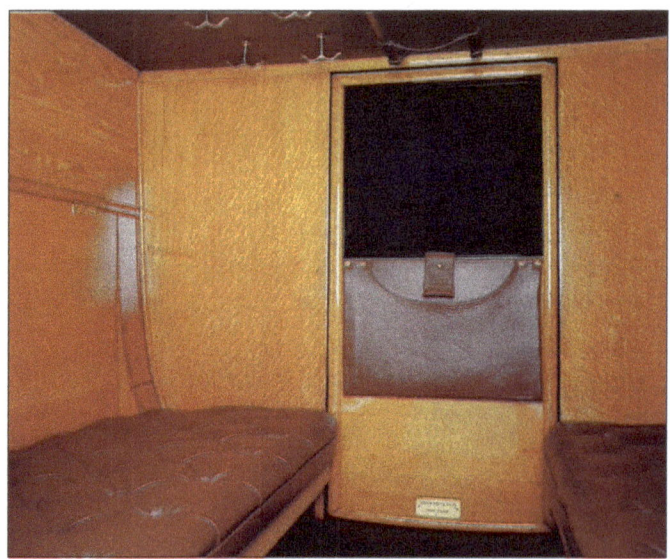

- Wood panels lined interior
- Cushions only on seat, often not on seat backs

APPOINTMENTS

For a Park Drag

- Period appropriate picnic supplies
- Food of the era for a tail gate picnic
- Hand straps
- Imperial
- Lamps
- Proper wheel wrench
- Aprons and lap robes and quarter sheets
- Proper rain wear for people including rain quarter sheets for horses
- Stick basket with umbrellas and walking sticks
- Horn sounder and horn case not necessary on a Park Drag and sounder can sound in seated position
- Driver's whip
- Invitation and seating cards
- *Driving on public roadways in current times requires a slow moving vehicle sign.

For a Road Coach

- Tools for repairs for travel
- Accessories for care of the horses
- Hand straps and longer one for horn sounder and possibly a horn case
- Stick basket for umbrellas, walking sticks, and horn.
- Luggage rack with leather straps
- Lamps sometimes adjustable so glass can be covered so not broken with daytime travel.
- Aprons and lap robes including rain wear for horses and people
- Proper hats on all passengers
- Coachman's whip
- Seats numbered
- *Driving on public roadways in current times requires a slow moving vehicle sign.

Park Drag Spares

Park drags were often driven in parks and places where there would be assistance if required. Therefore there are not as many items in the spares kit as in the Road Coach.

- Spare whip
- Lead and Side Bar
- Trace
- Rein and Trace Splice
- Hame Strap
- Bit
- Wheel Wrench
- Halter and Leads for horses
- Hoof pick
- Hole punch
- Cord or "Slough String" and Wire
- Extra Kidney Link

Road Coach Spares

Road Coaches were driven distances of eight to twelve miles. There was no assistance available on the route so they needed to carry whatever they may need for repairs.

- Spare whip
- Lead and Side Bar
- Trace
- Rein
- Hame Strap
- Bit
- Wheel Wrench
- Oil Can
- Grease Bucket
- Leather Water Buckets
- Halters and Leads for horses
- Portable Lantern with candle
- Quarter Sheets
- Spare Bridle
- Hoof Pick
- Horse Shoes and Nails
- Brake Block
- Kidney Link
- Straw Collar
- Nose Bags and Feed
- Hole Punch
- Cord or Rawhide
- Hole Punch
- Cord or "Slough String" and Wire

Stick baskets are located on the near side of the coach and the horn case on the offside.

The spares kit is on the floor of the interior in a Park Drag and in the boot of a Road Coach. The spares kit can be located in either location on a Private Road Coach depending on the configuration of the Private Road Coach. The boot of the Park Drag is equipped with china, crystal and cold food and beverages. The hot food chest is carried on the floor of the interior of the coach.

COACHES AND COACHING THROUGHOUT THE AGES

COACHES IN FRANCE

French coach, about 1640

The French, too, had a rich heritage of carriage building.

Carrosse of Henri IV of France, 1610

Parisian three-horse fiacre, *about* 1650

The English would call this turnout, of one horse in front of another, a "unicorn" after the mythological horse with a horn on its forehead.

French dormeuse *traveling carriage, about* 1840

This Cee Spring traveling coach is driven postilion with riders (Post Boys) on the near horses. The occupants of this carriage could stretch out and sleep by converting the seat into a bed.

COACHES AND COACHING THROUGHOUT THE AGES

The Berline

French berline-coupée (post chaise), about 1770

The double perch characterizes a Berline. The carriage only consists of the rear section for two forward facing passengers. No one other than the coachman would be obstructing their view. This early Coach (c. 1770) body is suspended from "S" shaped metal springs projecting from each of the two perches connecting the rear axle to the front of this Berline. It was developed in Germany. Glass windows, to keep the weather out, appeared in carriages about 1680.

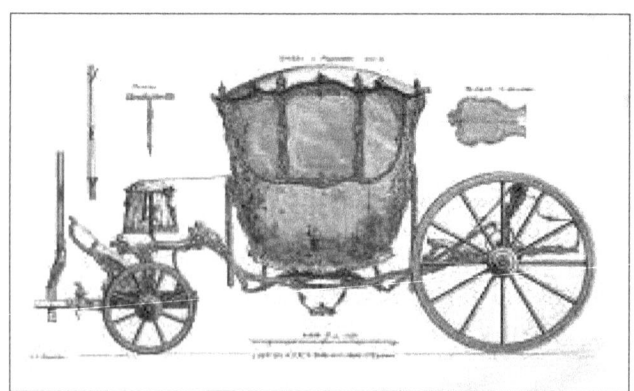

THE DILIGENCE

The diligence, a larger vehicle pulled by five horses, was common on the continent of Europe. The post boy is riding the near wheel horse (ride horse) to leave more room on the coach for cargo. One post boy is driving five horses.

Driving five horses in breast-collar harness to a large Diligence was not uncommon on the continent of Europe. The British drove four horses in full-collar harness to their English style coaches.

COACHES AND COACHING THROUGHOUT THE AGES

Light weight, strong materials were sought to lighten the weight of these heavy, large coaches. This Diligence has a lighter weight basket weave in front and back.

St. Moritz was a popular health resort destination in the late 1800s. Guests arrived at the resort via a Diligence.

The large diligence is iconic in France and immortalized the inns and taverns where they stopped.

Contemporary Diligence

Gala Coaches

While owner-driven vehicles remained relatively simple, the state coach only became more ornate.

This is an Imperial Carriage. It dates from the Baroque period and was used for coronations and other important ceremonies at the imperial court in Vienna.

This is the Coronation Carriage of Catherine the Great of Russia. It was used by her in 1762. It was ordered by Peter the Great and built in France. The side panels were painted by the French Rococo court painter Francois Boucher.

This full state carriage is called a coupe which means a cut-off coach without the front interior seat facing backwards. It weighs three thousand eight hundred pounds and can be pulled by four, six, or eight horses. It was manufactured by Armbruster of Vienna in the mid to late 1800s.

It was owned by the Imperial Hapsburg family of Emperor Franz Joseph and Empress Elizabeth, nicknamed "Sisi." It and other similar carriages were used for high ranking individuals for special occasions such as weddings, coronations, and other gala or full-dress affairs.

This full state carriage is currently owned by Gloria Austin.

Full state harness adorned with crowns and with extra ornamentation would have been appropriate. Full state livery would be worn.

AMERICA GETS ITS COACHES

Before the arrival of carriages and coaches America needed two very important things that Europe had but America did not have yet...*ROADS and HORSES*

The Oldest Carriage House

IN THE UNITED STATES.

J. B. BREWSTER & CO.,

145 East 25th Street, New York.

Sole Makers of the "BREWSTER WAGON" with Vertical Steel Plates in Axle Beds, which stiffens the axles, causing the wheels to run plumb.

NEW WAREROOMS, - - 489 FIFTH AVENUE.

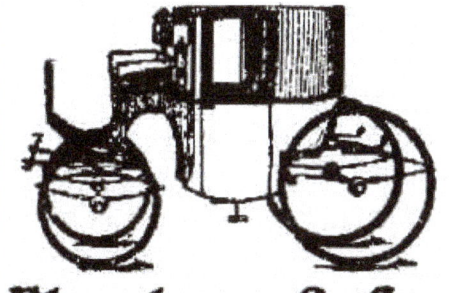

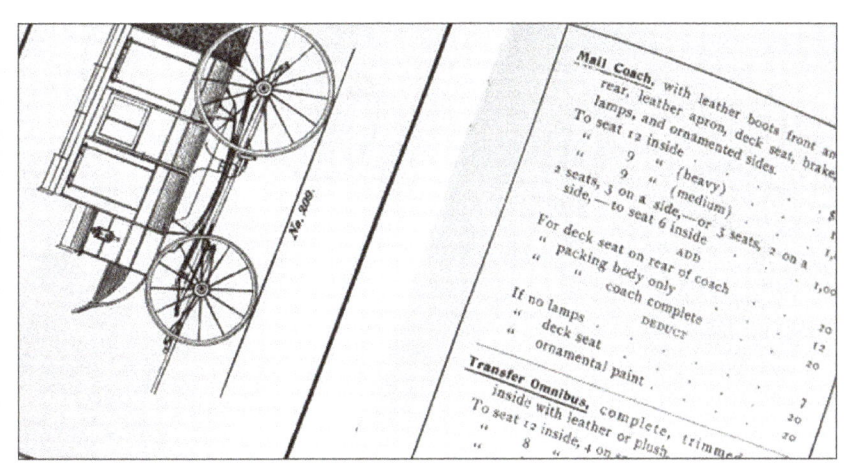

The Horse Had To Get There First

Most people are not aware that five hundred years ago there were thousands of bison, deer, and dogs in North America; but no cattle, hogs, or horses. These animals had to come from Europe with the early explorers and eventually early settlers or colonists.

Queen Isabella of Spain mandated Columbus to bring horses to the New World. His cargo on his second voyage in 1494 included approximately twenty quality military mounts and five mares along with cattle, sheep, pigs, goats and chickens to set up a European type community across the ocean on the island of Hispaniola.

Forty horses and horsemen arrived on his third voyage. The quest for gold resulted in the spreading of European culture and diseases to the New World in exchange for foods and other discoveries on which Europe learned to depend.

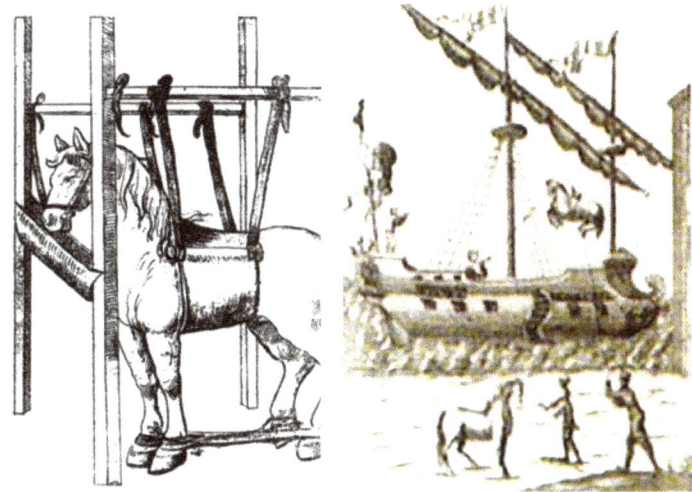
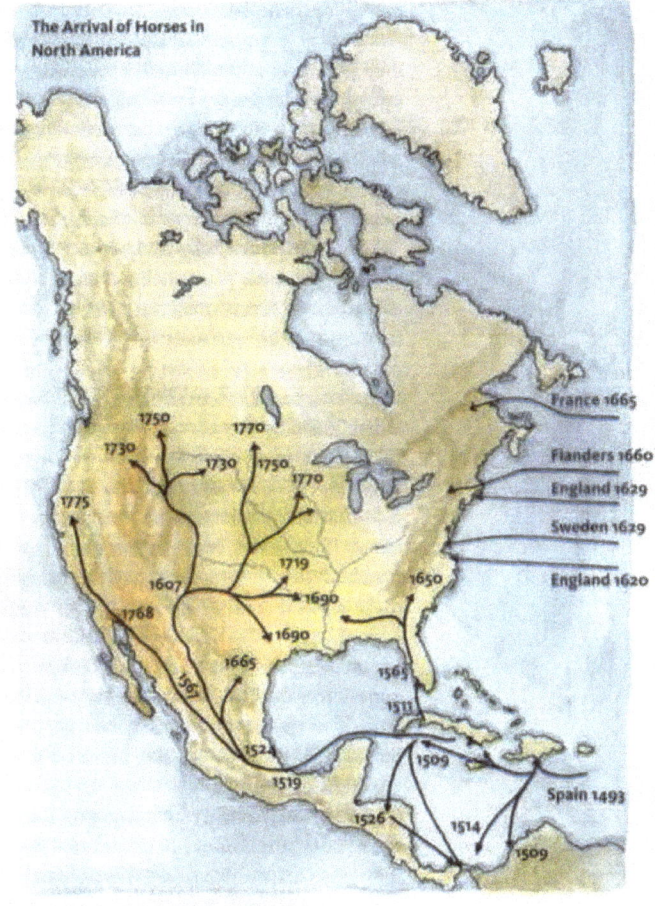

The crossing of the Atlantic was very dangerous and perilous. Some of the first crossings took fifty to seventy-five days of sailing.

The horses were shipped in the dark and damp hold of the ship. They were placed in slings to take the weight off their feet and prevent them from slipping and falling in rough seas.

With almost no exercise, the crossing was not suited to the horse's basic nature.

There is a section of the Atlantic known as the "Horse Latitudes" where many dead horses were thrown overboard. Between twenty-five and fifty percent died in transit.

Later, voyages gave way to transport on the top level of the boat to avoid the stench and debris gathered below from the horse's urine and manure.

ROADS AND CARRIAGES

Travel by natural waterways took many days even though many inland towns were only eight miles apart. Roadways in the Eastern United States grew from the need to travel shorter distances by land from settlement to settlement. It was a comfortable distance to travel by land for a horse before it needed to be rested or watered.

In France, Pierre-Marie-Jérôme Trésaguet and Telford and McAdam of Scotland were widely credited with establishing modern road building in the late 1700s.

For the comfort of passengers and the integrity of the body of coaches, hard surface roads were a necessity. Iron creates a stiffer, heavier suspension than the leather thoroughbraces, but roads had to improve in America before the widespread use of iron springs could provide the integrity needed for the coach bodies and comfort of the passengers.

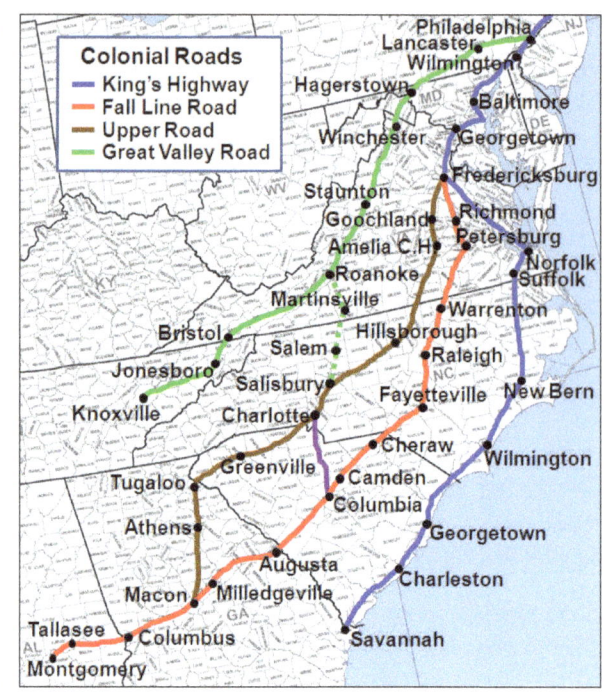

Roads, carriages and coaches had to be developed concurrently for comfort and speed to make travel desirable. The macadamizing of the roads in the United States in 1823 made it possible for stagecoaches to travel at much greater speeds.

In a seemingly short period of time, America transformed from a wilderness into a booming and bustling new country. Roads connected towns and stagecoaches traveled between the towns.

The Waterloo Inn was along the first stage between Baltimore and Washington. George Washington stopped here several times. Weather and bad roads made travel in America difficult and uncomfortable in the 1790's.

The coach house and the coach compartment of the stable at George Washington's home in Mount Vernon housed the family coach and a lighter vehicle, a chaise, which was a two-wheeled chair. From 1768 until the end of his life, Washington maintained a succession of fashionable carriages. None of them exist today.

The Powel coach, at Mt. Vernon, 1798

COACHES AND COACHING THROUGHOUT THE AGES

The coachee was generally a private vehicle used in the colonies of the United States. With no glass, passengers were protected in bad weather by side curtains that are seen here rolled up to the roof. The cee springs front and back with leather thoroughbraces protected the body of the coach and the passengers from the jar of the road surface.

American coachee, about 1795

The American public "Socialable" was for public use and had windows and a rack for luggage and parcels on its roof. As roads improved, so did suspension systems on the coaches and carriages. The Socialable was suspended on cee springs.

The heavier body of a Clarence is perched atop four Elliptic Springs.

Westward Ho!

As the country grew people headed west to start a new life. There were several routes to get to the west and, once there, people needed to travel from town to town and state to state just like they did in England.

Railroads did not destroy the stage line business like it did in Europe though. Vehicles of all types and sizes were needed around the railroad heads to transport goods and people through the vast lands of the west. There were over forty different types of vehicles in use and over three thousand Concord coaches were made.

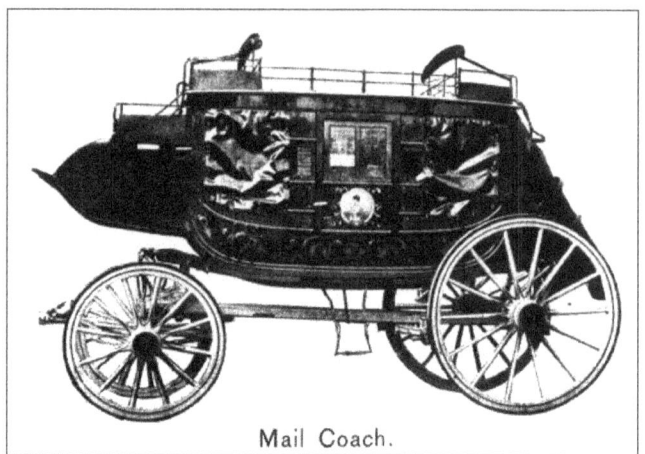
Mail Coach.

No. 220.

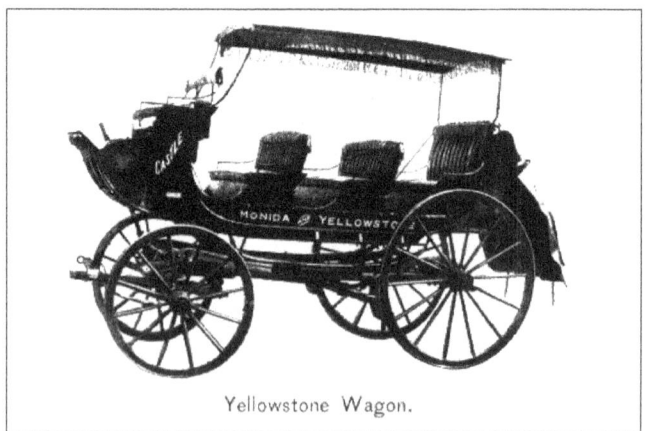
Yellowstone Wagon.

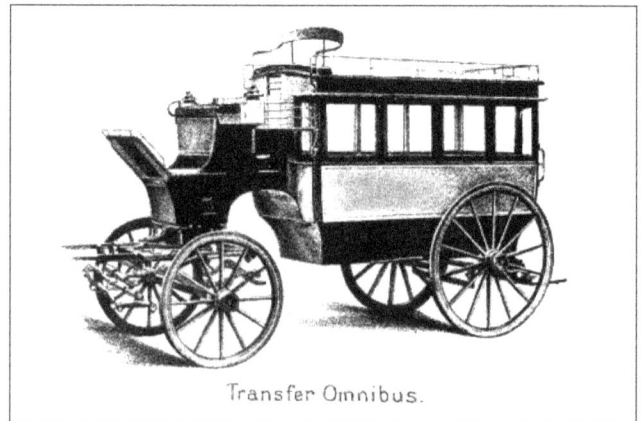
Transfer Omnibus.

The iconic American stagecoach was made in the Eastern United States in Concord, New Hampshire by the company Abbot and Downing. Wells Fargo Bank immortalized this image in its logo.

Passengers were told to, "expect annoyance, discomfort and hardships. If you are disappointed, thank heaven." Passengers sat knee to knee inside. They were allowed only a bit of luggage. They were told to expect motion sickness inside the coach. The mail had first priority to be inside if the weather was bad. It was a grand adventure intermixed with fear.

COACHES AND COACHING THROUGHOUT THE AGES

The Golden Age And The Gilded Age

Throughout history, times of great prosperity and enlightenment had been designated as the Golden Age. Such a time preceded the Civil War in the United States.

By 1857, carriage production had reached seven thousand carriages valued at 1.1 million dollars and New Haven, Connecticut was established as a carriage making center. Southern markets were open and mass production and steam power were at work.

The Civil War ended the boom and created a need for more specialization. G. D. Cook and Company were doing a better business by producing guns, knapsacks and shoes than when they were making carriages.

There was a steady decline in carriage production over the next ten years. The main vehicle for getting about in the city for the less wealthy, turned out to be the horsecar – a horse pulling a trolley car on tracks. The self propelled rail car was on its way.

Manifest Destiny, the telegraph and the railroad fueled the Gilded Age in America when the super wealthy wanted to replicate the British coaching ways.

The turnpike opened up the northeast. Steam engines and canals widened the scope of settlement in the East and West. However, it was the railroad that completed the picture. It was what brought the east and west coasts together.

Railroads helped to develop the western states by providing a safe means of reaching them. It brought to life the concept of Manifest Destiny, the idea that the United States truly was supposed to be a great nation reaching from the Atlantic Ocean to the Pacific Ocean.

By 1840, the United States was on track to have the greatest number of railroads in the world, doubling the three thousand miles of track in Europe. Twenty years later in 1860, the United States had constructed more than thirty thousand miles of railroad track.

This was not the end of the carriage business. Instead, the growth and shift of the population enhanced the need for wagons, coaches and carriages to get to and from the railheads. The railroad and the need for steel along with banking, made a wealthy class that wanted the best carriages and best carriage horses. Before income tax and government regulations, a group of the most prosperous were called "The Robber Barons." The Gilded Age was born.

In United States history, The Gilded Age was the period following the Civil War, running from the late 1860s to about 1896 when the next era, the Progressive Era, began. The term was coined by writers Mark Twain and Charles Dudley Warner in "The Gilded Age: A Tale of Today", which satirized what they believed to be an era of serious social problems obscured by a thin veneer of prosperity. The Gilded Age was a time of enormous growth that attracted millions of European immigrants. Railroads were the major industry but the factory system, mining, and labor unions also gained in importance.

During the 1870s and the 1880s, the U.S. economy rose at the fastest rate in its history with real wages, wealth, gross domestic product (GDP) and capital formation all increasing rapidly. Between 1865 and 1898, the output of wheat increased by 256%, corn by 222%, coal by 800% and miles of railway track by 567%. National networks for transportation and communication were created.

The corporation became the dominant form of business organizations and a managerial revolution transformed business operations. By the beginning of the 20th century, per capita income and industrial production in the United States led the world, with per capita income doubling that of Germany or France and 50% higher than Britain. (cited from: The Golden Age: 1860–1932." Boundless Political Science. Boundless, 21 Jul. 2015. Retrieved 25 Dec. 2015)

Power-hungry politicians and entrepreneurs emerged to create a class of super-rich industrialists and financiers such as Cornelius Vanderbilt, John D. Rockefeller, Andrew W. Mellon, Andrew Carnegie, Henry Flagler and J.P. Morgan. They all wanted beautiful homes, beautiful horses, beautiful carriages and grand large coaches. For instance, the Webb property in Shelburne, Vermont was created from  more than thirty separate farms on the shores of Lake Champlain and is known today as Shelburne Farms. The property is a National Historic Landmark and one of the main concert sites of the Vermont Mozart Festival. The former Webb estate has stunning views and some of the grandest barns of any Gilded Age property. Dr. Webb, a great horseman, had a large collection of carriages, many of which are on display today at the Shelburne Museum. William Seward Webb, a medical doctor, married Eliza Osgood Vanderbilt and was an entrepreneur, a financier and a gentleman farmer. For thirty years, the Webbs lived at 680 Fifth Avenue, New York. A long stretch of Fifth Avenue, including the home of the Webbs (below), was called Vanderbilt Row since so many family members lived in the various mansions. Their house, a wedding gift from William H. Vanderbilt to his daughter, was sold in 1913 to John D. Rockefeller.

THE WEALTHY IN THE GILDED AGE

- Andrew Carnegie: Railroads and Steel
- John D. Rockefeller: Oil
- Commodore Cornelius Vanderbilt: Shipping and Railroads
- John Jacob Astor: Real Estate and Fur
- Henry Clay Frick: Steel
- Jay Gould and James Fisk: Railroads and Finance
- Andrew Mellon: Finance
- Leland Stanford: Railroads
- John Pierpont Morgan: Finance
- Collis P. Huntington: Railroads
- Charles Crocker: Railroads
- George Mortimer Pullman: Railroads

During the Gilded Age, America changed radically. After the westward expansion of the railroad and telegraph, the display of wealth manifested itself in the use of the Park Drag and Private Road Coaches in America.

Fairman Rogers

Fairman Rogers (1835-1900) wrote the definitive book on coaching in America and is credited with the introduction of four-in-hand driving in Philadelphia. He was a Professor of Engineering at the University of Pennsylvania. He was the co-founder of the University of Pennsylvania's School of Veterinary Medicine. He served on the special trustees committee that recommended the school's establishment in 1884. Penn Vet is the only veterinary school in the United States that was a direct outgrowth of the University's School of Medicine and is one of the world's premier veterinary schools. Penn Vet has led the way in such areas as infectious disease research, germ cell biology, animal trans-genesis, comparative oncology and comparative medical genetics.

The Fairman Rogers Four-in-Hand

COACHES AND COACHING THROUGHOUT THE AGES

The Penn Libraries have one thousand items from Rogers' library and has digitized the Fairman Rogers collection of books on horses and horsemanship. A scrapbook, diary and twenty-seven of his letters and notes are found in The Union League Library on Broad Street in Philadelphia. The Union League is a private members only club founded in 1862 to support the policies of Abraham Lincoln. Rogers was one of its founding members.

In 1899, Rogers' "A Manuel of Coaching" was published and is mandatory reading for enthusiasts of coaches and driving. This five hundred seventy-nine page book has twenty-seven chapters and many valuable illustrations. The following is a listing of some of the subjects covered:

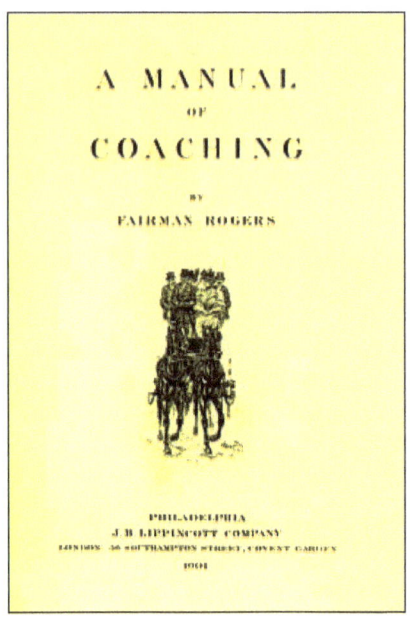

General Character of a Coach
- Accessories
- Types of Carriages and Coaches
- Harness
- Harnessing and Putting-to
- Driving, Including Methods of Fingering
- Horses for Coach or Drag
- Whip and Its Use
- Public Coaching
- Coaching Trips
- Rules of the Road
- Accidents
- Clubs
- Music for the Horn

On Fifth Avenue, the carriages, Lady's Phaetons, Coaches and even Tubs would pass one another. Stock would be taken of a new hat, new livery, new coach, a new beau. It was called society's "dress parade" - a time to take the measure of one another. It was also society's daily meet and greet to find out who was in town and who was not, who was under the weather and who was in the pink. There was even a four-in-hand society for women. The women were on the road too in their great coaches with all riders on the top to see and be seen. (cited from: https://theberkshireedge.com/connections-coaching-and-driving-in-the-gilded-age/)

References to coaching were seen everywhere. Even clothing manufacturers included coaches in their advertising. If you wanted to be seen flaunting your new style, then the top of a coach was the place to be!

Anne Morgan (daughter of J.P. Morgan) and
Harriet Alexander (wife of Charles B. Alexander
and daughter of Charles Crocker)

Exhibiting Coaches with Four-in-Hands at horse shows also became very popular and prestigious.

In June 1907, the first International Horse Show held in London, opened its doors to the public. Over five hundred horses including many from the Continent of Europe were entered. Even wealthy sporting American patrons brought their horses over from the United States. The catalogue detailed all classes, entries and prizes and gave a full list of each day's musical performance. Alfred Vanderbilt had the winning Road Team and also winner of twenty-three other first prizes.

CHAMPION FOUR-IN-HAND TEAM OF THE WORLD.
WHEELERS—VENTURE, VIKING.   LEADERS—VANITY, VOGUE.
OWNED BY MR. ALFRED G. VANDERBILT.

The Park Drag of Mr. A. W. Atkinson driven by John Goodwin

Mrs. Loula Long Combs driving her park four

William H. Moore's Road Four as shown at the National Capital Horse Show in Washington, D. C.

J. Campbell Thomas with his Road Four. Winners of the Vanderbilt Memorial Challenge Cup class at Madison Square Garden in 1915

Putting Together A Coach and Four

Harnessing

Four-in-hand harness has all the components of two sets of pair harness with the following additions. The wheel pads have center terrets that have the usual bearing rein hook and above it a ring to carry the lead reins. The wheelers bridles also have terrets for the leader reins. Often this terret is mounted on the outside rosette of the bridle. The lead reins are obviously longer than the wheeler reins. The coupling reins are about the same length as those on the wheel reins.

The hames with the ring on the anchor and fixed dee are the types for a road Coach. The fixed hame anchor and jointed hame dee is for a Park Drag.

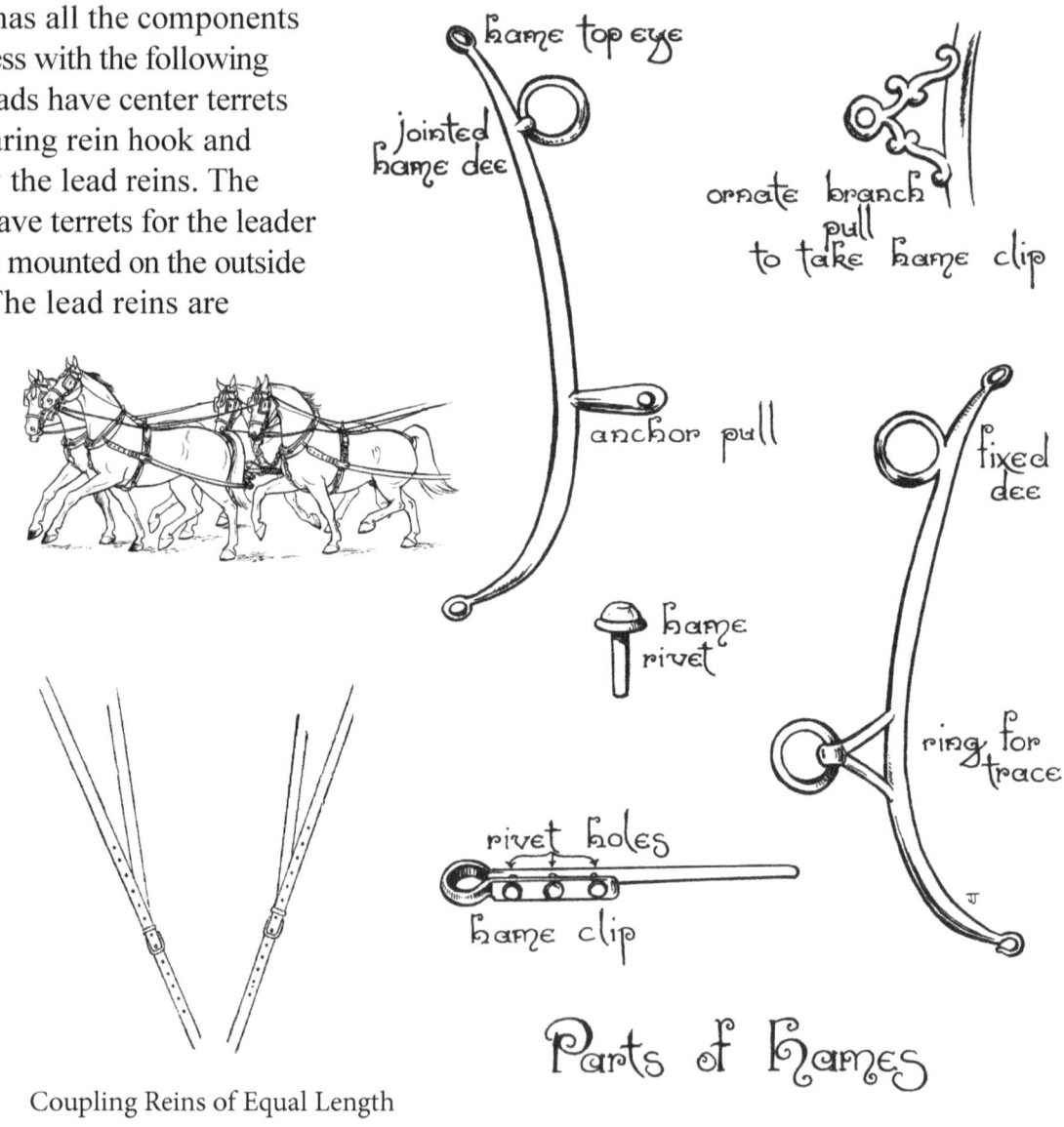

Coupling Reins of Equal Length

Parts of Hames

The lead traces have cock eyes on the ends that are used for attaching the traces to the hooks on the swingletrees.

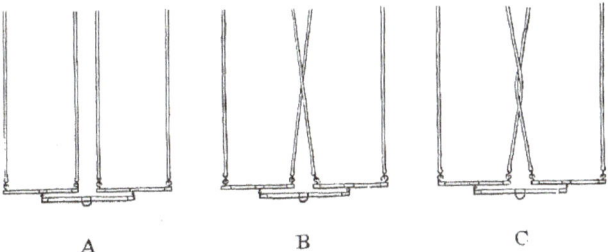

A - is an image of traces attached directly to the sidebars.
B - is an image of crossed traces which should not be used in coaching, only perhaps when training.
C - is an image of lapped traces which is recommended for coaching and driving a four to lighter carriages. In coaching, the leaders are not connected at the collars, as is the case in combined driving.
This system of lapping the traces helps to keep the leaders together when coaching.

Combined drivers use the connecting strap at the collars to prevent the leaders from going either side of a tree or post.

Park Drag harness is black and is lighter with a finer finish than Road Coach harness. The back pads on the Park Drag harness are straight and trimmed with patent leather and the blinkers should be square or "D" shape. A crest or monogram may be on the blinkers, face pieces, and breastplates. The metal on the harness should match the metal on the coach and Buxton bits are used on the horses.

COACHES AND COACHING THROUGHOUT THE AGES

COACH HORSES

There would be no coaching without horses!

At first, horses of all sizes and types were used for coaches depending on the type of coach. As Coaching became a sport more than a necessity, breeding of horses specifically for coaching became important.

Horses used for Mail Coaches and Stage Coaches were not specifically bred for that purpose; any horse that could do the job was used to pull the coaches. Fairs and markets were common and the horse trading business was a major component of the economy. Often horses that were "bad actors" could be purchased for a reasonable price and, once put with other horses in a hitch and asked to work, the horse became a cooperative, hard worker.

Many types of horses were used in a Stagecoach team in the early American colonies too: runaways, kickers, biters and tricksters. If the owners couldn't manage them they went on Stagecoaches. They were seldom sick, were well fed and groomed, and had quick times; it is said that they never died! (cited from: Stagecoach Days by Pat Tafra)

Royal Mail meeting strings of horses being taken to a Fair

Even nowadays the Queen of England's Windsor Grays are not a particular breed, but rather, any gray that is specifically bred and subsequently selected by the Royals to join the official ranks. Their selection is based primarily on temperament and appearance, as their singular duty is pulling or accompanying the Queen's Coach. The horses are saddle trained before they are carriage trained, and should you ever feel like taking a walk in St. James's Park at around five in the morning, you may see the Grays getting an early morning hack in downtown London. (cited from: https://www.horse-nation.com/2012/04/02/horses-in-history-britains-royal-mews/)

In the days of the Mail Coach and Stagecoaches, often a light horse (white or gray) was positioned in the lead to be seen at night.

Despite weather conditions, the coaches ran where one could barely see the way. The drivers were skillful and the horses had to be reliable in a storm and keen about remembering the way.

Horse and Carriage by David Dalby of York

Delivery of the mail was so important that when coaches became stuck in snow drifts it was imperative to continue the journey on horseback in order to deliver the mail and seek assistance. The horses had to be ready to ride when necessary and needed to be calm while waiting for assistance.

Mail Coach in a Thunder Storm on New Market

Mail Coach in a Snow Drift by James Pollard

Horses needed to stand quietly and be ready to make a quick change at the coach stops - so quick that the passengers did not even get off of the coach. The putting-to process had to be done by skilled grooms to make sure every detail was accounted for. The same was true of the unhitching. Mistakes could be costly to property and life if a horse were to get frightened and become unruly.

As Coaching became a sport more than a necessity, breeding of horses specifically for coaching became important.

Cleveland Bays (named for the Cleveland District of Yorkshire, England) are considered the oldest non-draft English breed. They were developed by the Church of England officials who needed a hardy but swift pack horse that could carry goods to more remote abbeys and monasteries in northeast England. They were mixtures of English drafts and Spanish Andalusians. Much later Thoroughbred and Arabian blood was added to make them a slightly taller and leggier horse for coaching. They are always bays in color. Despite their popularity and beloved royal status, the Cleveland Bay is extremely rare with approximately five hundred purebreds in the world. They are found in the foundational lineage of some of today's popular breeds including Oldenburg, Holstein, and Hanoverian. (cited from: https://www.horsenation.com/2012/04/02/horses-in-history-britains-royal-mews/)

Cleveland Bay

The Yorkshire Coach Horse (now extinct) was a large, strong, bay or brown horse. It was said to have an unmatched ability for a combination of speed, style, and power and was tall, and elegant. With the introduction of macadamized roads, the Cleveland Bay horse was considered not fast enough and as a result, some Cleveland Bays were bred to Thoroughbred horses to produce the Yorkshire Coach Horse.

Breaston Prince
a Yorkshire Coach horse

COACHES AND COACHING THROUGHOUT THE AGES

Many breeds used now for dressage and jumping were initially bred using heavy coaching horses. Nearly every country in Europe made use of the English bred carriage horses as a foundation for

Norfolk Trotter

their Warmbloods. The Hanoverians and Holsteiners and nearly every German breed, except the Trakehner, are descendants of the Yorkshire Coach horses and Norfolk Trotters from the 19th century. These English horses were bred with heavy cold-blooded German horses to produce the "warmbloods". (cited from: http://home.claranet.nl/users/lijssel/nederlnd/The%20Origins%20of%20the%20Warmblood%20Horse.htm)

White Hanoverian Leader

As the status of Coaching grew, the desire for quality horses increased. Having a color-matched team of horses was essential for driving a Park Drag.

Gloria Austin driving various matched teams with a Park Drag.

DRIVING A FOUR-IN-HAND

The British style of driving has been preserved for a long time. Every wealthy man (and some women) wanted to demonstrate their skill at driving four horses by holding four reins in their left hand, while using the right hand for the whip and manipulating the reins. This British coachman style was promulgated in Hints on Driving by Captain C. Morley Knight.

The Germans so loved this style that Achenbach studied with the British coachman, Edwin Howlett. He returned to Germany and promulgated this style of driving for the German military.

Benno von Achenbach studied with Howlett.

The British style of driving is one of many types used around the world to drive three, four or more horses to large carriages. Russia had the unique Troika to drive three horses. Germany and other Eastern European counties use a Hungarian system which often included five horses but failed to have the precision of the British style. The French and Americans used slightly differing techniques. The focus in the following pages is on the British style or driving four horses to an English style coach.

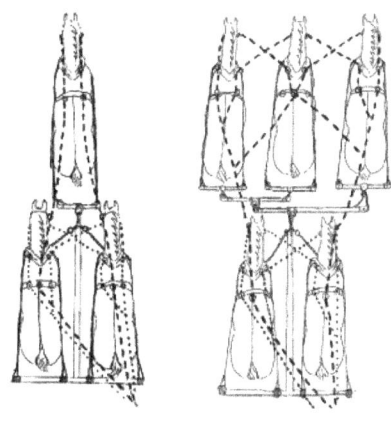

Unicorn   Pickaxe

Four-in-hand driving is used for tandem, unicorn, and driving a Pickaxe. With all of these configurations there are four reins that feed back to the driver's hand.

With the Pickaxe the leaders have two sets of coupling reins – one set is in the typical position for a pair but connects to the middle horse, and the other set joins the outside or long rein at the top of the outside horse's hips as shown in the diagram at the lower right and connect to each outside horse.

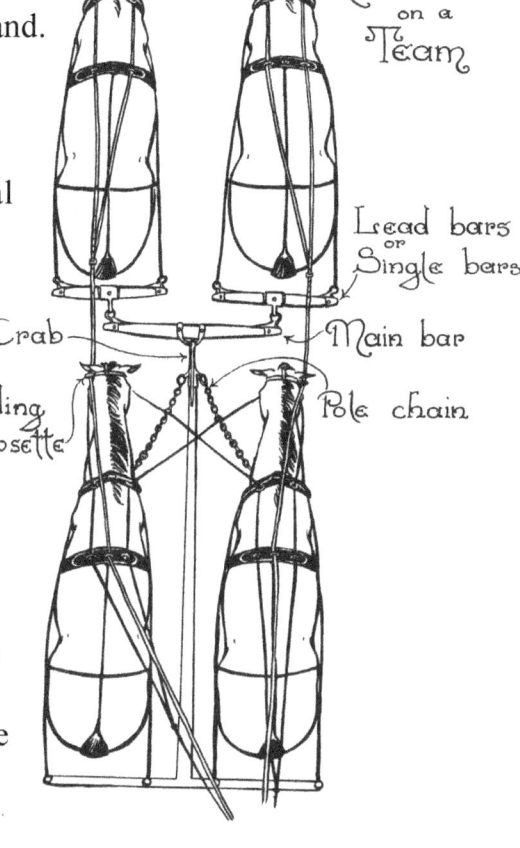

Details of Reins & Bars on a Team

Lead bars or Single bars
Crab
Main bar
Leading eye rosette
Pole chain

Team

Drivers have to be aware of the distance the inside and outside reins have to be moved during the process of the turn. With a tandem, the reins that connect to each horse are only as far apart as the single horse's bit, whereas the outside reins for the three abreast are three horses apart. In the case of the pair, it is only two horses apart. This means the driver must be aware of the amount of pull and distance the reins have to travel to activate a turn.

This precision driving through the city streets of London and on the roadways throughout Great Britain aided in controlling and directing four horses put to three thousand pound coaches laden with mail, passengers and parcels.

The two pairs of horses are driven around corners, one set at a time – turning the lead pair and then the wheel pair.

COACHES AND COACHING THROUGHOUT THE AGES

The reins are held in the left hand and the whip in the right hand. The reins are manipulated by the right hand and left hand, often simultaneously, which require special skill while still holding the whip and occasionally tapping a wheel horse with the stick or the lead horse with the lash.

A system of gathering and letting loops slide through the fingers signal each of the two pairs of horses to bend and either go straight, follow their heads or do lateral movements to either the right or left.

The whip is used to signal the horses, salute or indicate turns, stopping or moving onward.

Driving a Four-in-Hand is very complex involving not only the taking and giving of loops, but rotations of the wrist, flexing of the finger and use of the arms, body and legs. Like all things done well, it must be learned and repeated many, many times to acquire the necessary skills and proficiency.

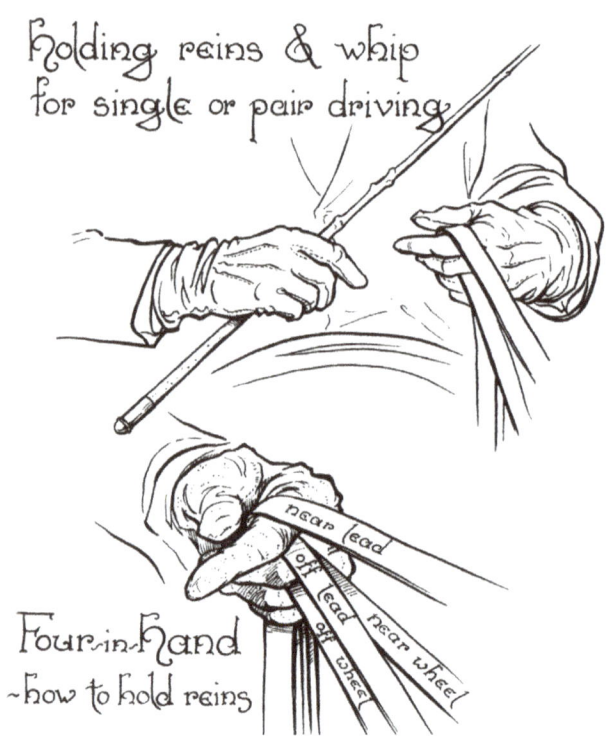

One important aspect of this type of driving is to hold the right hand close to the left for a quicker response in directing the horses and also to keep track of each rein without looking down at one's hands. The driver must stay focused on the horses to anticipate their movement and take corrective action.

The whip (driver) covers the left hand with the right which puts him/her in position to follow the desired rein forward without looking down at his/her hands when selecting the rein or reins the whip (driver) wishes to touch and activate.

The horses are signaled with the reins, voice and/or whip to look in the direction of the turn, then follow their heads and/or do lateral movements to travel on a precise path of the driver's intention.

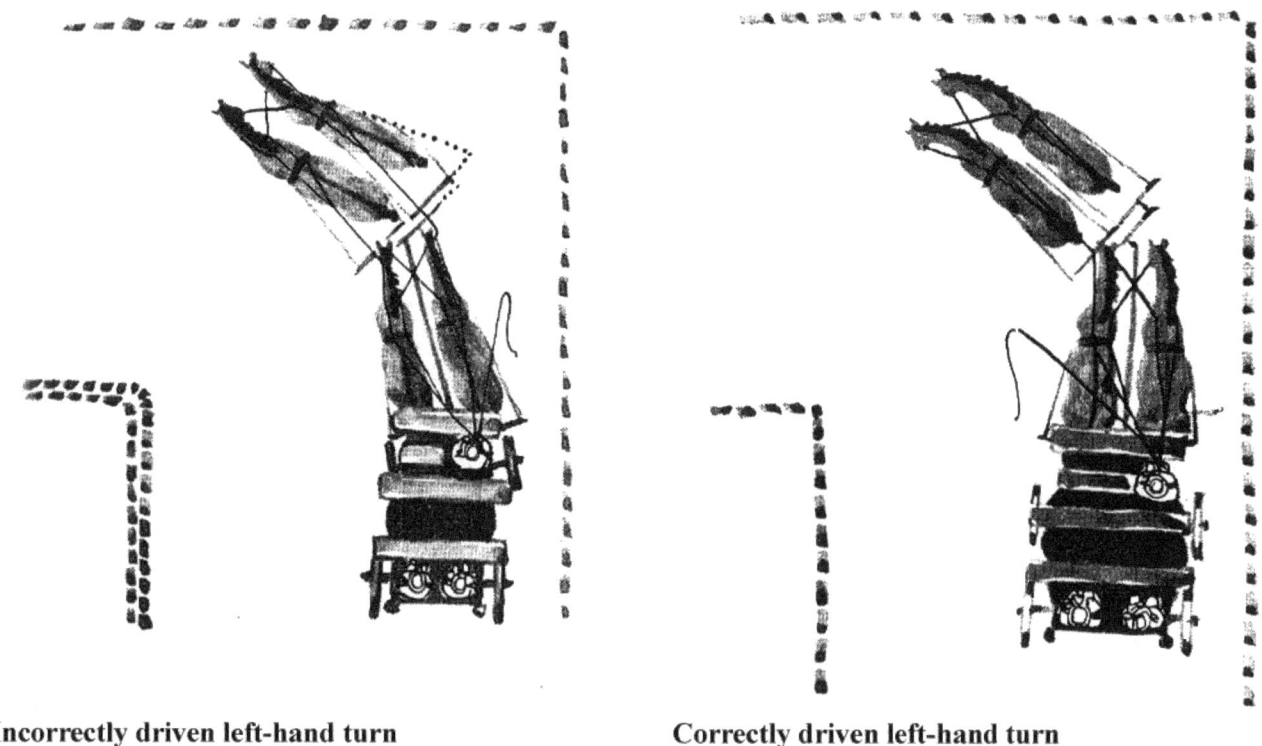

Incorrectly driven left-hand turn   **Correctly driven left-hand turn**

For a left turn, the whip takes or picks the loop with the thumb and index finger and holds the whip at the butt end so when reaching to make a loop, the end of the whip does not get caught on any of the three reins in the left hand. The taking of a rein is often done with an ever so slight tug (half-halt) to direct the pair of horses to bend to the left. The right hand remains close to the left hand to be used quickly and frequently.

For a right turn, the whip takes the right loop in the same fashion as the left and places that loop between the thumb and index finger of the left hand. Once these loops are drawn there may be a necessity to reach a second time to make the loop bigger for a tighter turn.

When the horse or horses are bent in the direction of the turn, the right hand is placed on the reins to the inside or outside of the turn to signal lateral movements either to the right or left. This allows the whip to direct the footfalls of each set of horses to move through gateways and around corners.

Clubbing the reins is the procedure of placing all reins in the left hand by placing the off reins on top of the hand with the index finger separating the off reins.

FIG. 138. POINT TO THE LEFT.
FIG. 146. STOPPING.
FIG. 140. POINT TO THE RIGHT.
FIG. 139. POINT TO THE LEFT.
FIG. 141. POINT TO THE RIGHT.

Four-in-hand reins

Close-up of reins for four-in-hand driving

A) Dead stop with left hand raised and reins taken by right hand in from left

B) Shortening near lead rein by taking back with right hand

C) Making loop to point leaders to the left by the overhand method

D) Pointing leaders to the right with the loop in off lead rein held under thumb

E) Making loop in off lead rein by underhand method

F) Turn to the left with near lead looped under thumb and opposition on off wheel rein made by passing it over thumb

From "On the Box Seat"
by Tom Ryder

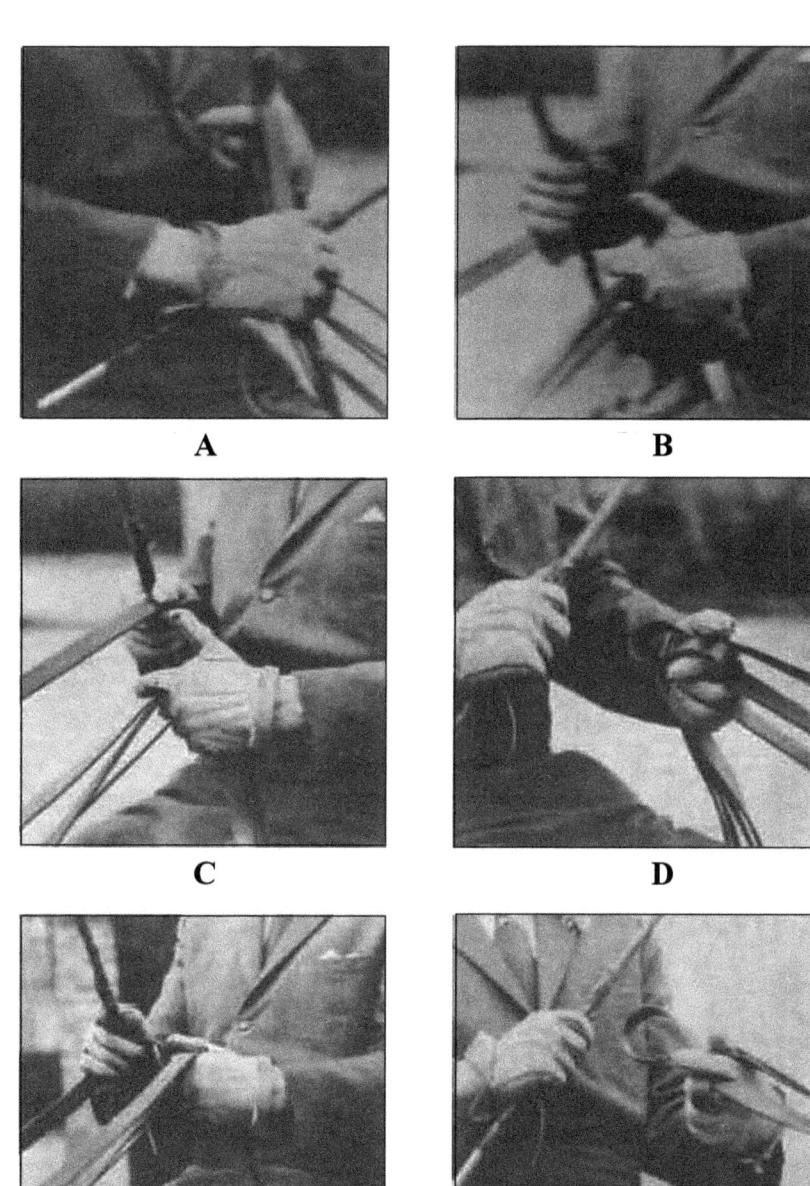

The voice is used for directing the horses but a whip is also essential. The four-in-hand bow whip of the English generally has an eight foot stick and twelve foot lash. The stick is made of a variety of woods, holly being the most sought after. Today light weight modern materials like carbon fiber are also used.

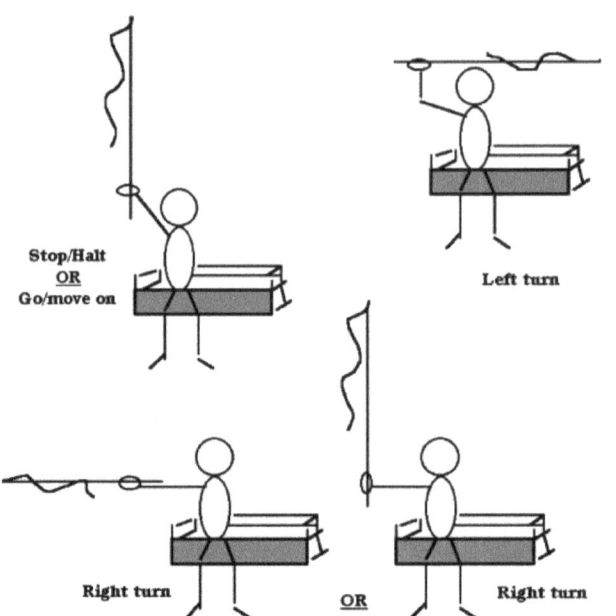

Fairman Rogers

The lash is of braided leather with a cracker (cotton string) at the end. Called a "cracker" since it makes a cracking noise when moving through the air faster than the speed of sound.

The whip is used in the right hand to signal turns by raising the whip and extending the arm, or to give the horse direction by taping the wheelers with the stick or unfurling the whip so the thong can reach the leaders . The whip is also used to salute in acknowledgment of another coach, a judge or person on the ground. The whip is transferred to the left hand and placed atop the reins to use the brake with the freed right hand, or for the man to lift his hat and salute, or to free the right hand for a hand shake. Unfurling, furling, and using the whip is an art that must be practiced.

Proper posture is important in order for the whip to balance on the box seat and use the reins and whip effectively.

The British Hand is also easily adaptable to driving with six reins - you just keep stacking. Six reins are held in the left hand and manipulated with both. The stacking system from top to bottom is left, right leaders; left, right swing pair; left, right wheelers.

Now, it becomes tricky to pick the correct rein, so it is imperative to keep the right hand close to feel which rein is which. Fortunately, a six-in-hand or six-up was used mostly on long straight roads like in our American West. Horses that are trained to go as a pair and four, adapt to being driven as six very readily. The difficulty is in making turns with any degree of precision.

COACHES AND COACHING THROUGHOUT THE AGES

ATTIRE

"No matter how perfect the finish of the carriage, nor how complete its appointments, the effect will be completely spoiled if certain essential matters have not received equal attention." Tom Ryder

The whip (driver) and passengers dress in conservative contemporary attire while the grooms are in "livery". Think of livery as a uniform worn by the grooms who are attending the horses, whip, passengers and carriage. The livery today is the same as it was in the coaching era.

The whip and box seat passengers normally wear driving aprons. The apron covers the lap and legs all the way down to the footwear. Passengers on the front and back Gamon seats normally wear lap robes. The lap robe is a boxy cut and is generally shorter than aprons and usually not fastened. Lap robes are designed to cover the laps and legs. Both aprons and robes should wrap about four inches above the waist.

Aprons and lap robes may be solid, checks or plaid and are made of seasonally appropriate weight. They do not need to match the color of the upholstery. Crests or monograms are to be positioned on the visible side of the aprons and in the center of the lap robes. Aprons and lap robes protect clothing from road dust and dirt.

The aprons and lap robes are appointments of the carriage and should be left with the carriage when passengers and whip dismount.

There are four classes of livery: Full State, Semi-State, Dress Livery, and Stable Livery

Full State Livery is used with state carriages and is now used primarily by royal households. The coachman sits on an ornate hammer-cloth, wearing a heavily decorated frock-coat.

The frock-coat for Semi-State Livery is single breasted and normally of the family color. The hat worn is a tall black hat with a cockade. The point at the top of the cockade indicates the status of the household for which the coachman is seated. The Ascot outrider wears a scarlet jacket.

These coachmen are in scarlet Ascot livery and black formal livery. Only the Queen's Coachmen are to have cream tops on their livery boots which are not as tall as riding boots and straight cut at their tops.

The guard, a vestige of the Mail Coach, protected the cargo and passengers from the highwaymen who would steal valuables from passengers and take unprotected cargo. The guard was the master of the ship in that he kept the time with a clock in the front of his pouch and, he also carried the weigh bills inside the pouch. The key to the boot could be found on the front of the pouch so he could easily access the mail and parcels carried on board. The scarlet uniform was a tradition in Great Britain, with white deerskin breeches and leggings over his paddock boots. He was a majestic figure atop the coach.

COACHES AND COACHING THROUGHOUT THE AGES

Years ago the coachman, often in full/dress livery, headed the wheel horses when stopped, sounded the horn and drove the horses when needed. He had to have all of these skills. Today, the coachman or coachwoman is in conservative attire and sits behind the driver and operates the brake on a heavy coach. In the case of an elderly driver the coachman or coachwoman sits beside the driver to assist if needed.

The coachman/coachwoman can also wear dress livery. The frock-coat should be in conservative stable colors or black with a velvet collar with six buttons at front and four at back. The coat should be at least six inches above the knee. He/she should wear a top hat, brown gloves and cream or white doeskin breeches. The boots should have brown boot cuffs. Hunt boots are not appropriate. A stock tie with stock pin or coach horn pin is also required. A senior groom would wear the same livery.

Dress livery for a groom would be the same except that the frock coat has five buttons at the front and six at the back.

Stable or casual livery consists of a jacket of tweed or solid dark colored, cap, tan trousers, brown gloves, brown paddock boots, white tie or dark tie. A groom in stable livery may also wear a bowler in which case the pants would be jods but still with paddock boots and a stock tie instead of a regular tie would be worn. A suit may also be worn for stable livery. It should be dark colored and a bowler would be worn along with a white shirt, dark tie and dark shoes. Stable livery is most appropriate on traveling tours with a Road Roach or Private Road Coach.

COACHING TODAY

Today there are clubs, organizations, associations museums, meets and shows to preserve coaching and carriage driving.

Clubs, Organizations, Associations and Museums

The New York Coaching Club was established in 1875 in New York City to encourage four-in-hand driving in America. The first English style coach was brought to America and driven in Boston in early 1860.

This Drag was displayed in the front room of Brewster & Company in New York City. It provided a fertile seed from which sprang the New York Coaching Club, an all-male club, known as The Coaching Club. The club still exists today.

The World Coaching Club was founded in 1983 by Cordelia Robinson, the founding President. It is open to women only from around the world.

(left) Mrs. Frank Hayden, founding member, driving the Wethersfield Hackney Horses at Newport

Coaches and Coaching Throughout the Ages

In 1856 the Marquis of Stafford chaired the Four-in-Hand Driving Club which was limited to thirty members, but increased to fifty under the presidency of the Eighth Duke of Beaufort.

Duke of Beaufort Leading Drive in Hyde Park about 1875

Newport Historical Society
Coaching Weekend

COACHES AND COACHING THROUGHOUT THE AGES

The Four-in-Hand Club was founded in the year 2000. It was the first club of its kind in history for both men and women. The Charter members were Gloria Austin, Jack Fairclouth, Dr. Gary Monsdeoca, Jack Wetzel, Sandy Lerner, John White, Micky Bowen, Hector Acalde and Frolic Weymouth. Membership requires: members own their own horses or ponies and drive in the traditional fashion of four reins in the left hand. Associate memberships are available to four-in-hand drivers who do not own their own turnout; these are mostly employed coachmen and coachwomen of full members.

In 1890 a Four-in-Hand Coaching Club was organized in the City of Philadelphia for those enthusiasts of the driving of four horses for pleasure. The Four-in-Hand Club of Philadelphia is a private organization whose object is to collect, preserve and perpetuate the history and traditions of Philadelphia coaching and the art of four-in-hand driving, as well as to promote the sport to its highest standards. In order to be eligible for the distinction of Coaching Member, the applicant must own a coach, or their immediate family must own a coach, and they must have driven a coach in a public setting in such a manner as to be considered "accomplished" in the estimation of the officers of the Club, who bestow such distinction.

Then

Now

Founded in 1960, the CAA was incorporated not-for-profit in 1962. It is the oldest and largest international organization devoted to the preservation and restoration of horse-drawn carriages and sleighs. The CAA established rules and guidelines for The Sporting Day of Traditional Driving (Attelage de Tradition) and offers Driving Proficiency Certificates. The association has three thousand members from thirty six countries and publishes "The Carriage Journal".

The American Driving Society was founded in 1974. The ADS establishes rules and guidelines for Pleasure Driving Shows and Combined Driving. They produce a Rule Book and Omnibus listing both Pleasure Driving Shows and Combined Driving Competitions as well as a magazine, "The Whip".

The Carriage Museum of America was incorporated as a not-for-profit educational institution in 1978. It serves as a library for historically accurate information on animal-drawn vehicles and related information. Their library is in Kentucky and their historic carriage collection is in Georgia.

COACHES AND COACHING THROUGHOUT THE AGES

Coaching Meets

Coaching meets are events organized for those who own and drive coaches and four-in-hands to gather and go on drives; usually several drives over several days. Picnics, dinners and parties are all part of the weekend. In 2004, The National Sporting Library in Middleburg, Virginia sponsored a meet that attracted thirty-three coaches. In 2007, the event attracted twenty-eight coaches. Other coaching meets that attract large numbers of participants are: The Berkshire Coaching Weekend hosted by Harvey and Mary Waller in Stockbridge, Massachusetts, a drive hosted by Joe Jennings in Monmouth County, New Jersey, The Big Bend hosted by Frolic Weymouth in Pennsylvania and the Newport Historical Society Coaching Weekend in Rhode Island.

Socializing on a coaching during a Meet.

The Preservation Society of Newport County recreates the sport of driving four horses to an English style coach every third year to raise funds for the preservation of the mansions of Newport. Gloria is one of a few women to be invited to this event and has presented her Healey Park Drag there on three occasions. Typically, only members of the New York Coaching Club are asked to drive at this prestigious event.

"Fairholme" (1874–1875) was Fairman Roger's summer cottage in Newport, Rhode Island . It was designed by Frank Furness. It is one of the many "cottages" built during the Gilded Age on beach front property in the Newport area.

Stabling for the event is at The Breakers, the summer home of Cornelius Vanderbilt II.

Shows

Currently, Devon in Pennsylvania, The Royal Winter Fair in Ontario, The Orleton Farm Show in Massachusetts and The Lexington Carriage Classic in Kentucky have Coaching Divisions. The Junior League Show in Lexington has one Coaching class but not a division for coaches. Classes offered in a division for coaching can include:

Turnout: Entries to be shown at an even trot, both ways of the ring. May walk when reversing across the diagonal and when lining up. Horses to stand quietly in the line-up. Judged on performance, quality, manners of the horses, and correct appointments.

Pleasure: Entries will be judged both ways of the ring at an even trot, and may walk when reversing across the diagonal and when lining up. Horses to stand quietly in the line-up. Judged on performance, quality, manners of the horses, and correct appointments.

Best Team: Entries to drive at a smart trot, both ways of the ring. May walk when reversing across the diagonal and when lining up. Horses to stand quietly in the line-up. Emphasis on overall impression and quality of the team and its performance.

Obstacles: Drivers negotiate, from memory, a course of paired markers.

Appointments: All appointments appropriate to the type of coach are judged.

Quick Change: A class designed to simulate the "quick change" of horses at an Inn - horses are unhooked, lead around a set of cones and then re-hitched. The entire procedure is timed.

Coach Horn: The horn player on the coach is judged for his/her ability while the coach is on the move.

November 22, 1922 was the date the first Royal Agricultural Winter Fair was held. The first coach entered the ring in 1963 as a demonstration organized by John A. McDougald. The whips were Frank & Cynthia Hayden who drove McDougald's Park Drag and Hackneys. They started coaching classes in 1964. The competition was called the Green Meadows Coaching Competition after McDougald's Green Meadows Farm.

Coaching With Gloria

Gloria Austin in Lexington, Kentucky

Gloria Austin at Walnut Hill

The "Quick Change" was designed to simulate the changing of horses at an inn or tavern when horses and large coaches were used for mail delivery and passenger travel. The coachman would pull up, the tired horse would be replaced by a set of fresh horses. Here in 2002, "Team Gloria" is seen setting the Walnut Hill record by removing horses and leading them around a set of cones before re-hitching in under two minutes. Milton Long joined Melissa Warner and David Saunders as part of the team that performed tasks in the proper order and without a twisted trace or rein.

Driving her famous blue Healey Coach, Gloria is shown here with Coachwoman, Melissa Warner, in Pittsford, New York at the Walnut Hill Farm Competition. Grooms are Kacy Tipton and Toni Jones. Held in August of each year, the five-day Walnut Hill Farm Driving Competition was America's premiere traditional driving event for 45 years. Present also on the coach is Horn Sounder, Dale Romagnoli on the rear Gamon seat and appointments coordinator, Linda Beaulieu on the front Gamon seat.

Mary and Harvey Waller sponsor The BerkshireCoaching Weekend in Stockbridge, Massachusetts in the Fall when the New England States are full of color. The Berkshire Mountains offer a backdrop unequaled.

COACHES AND COACHING THROUGHOUT THE AGES

After winning four-in-hand and coaching championship in the USA and Canada in 1998, Gloria took horses, carriages and staff to tour Europe which included participating in an Attelage de Tradition. These competitions are one-day driving shows with antique carriages. The three phases of this event include: Presentation at three stations, Routier over a course of about fifteen miles, and Maniabilité which is through 20 sets of cones.

Started by Christian and Antoinette de Langlad, these events have become popular throughout Europe. Gloria drove a Guiet coach once owned by the Bugatti family. Gloria drove this coach back in France one hundred years after it was manufactured in France in 1899. She is seen with Coachman Jean Paul Gautier, a Canadian originally from France.

There is always an opportunity to wear pearls. Sometimes the parties, particularly those at Newport, overshadow the coaching event itself. Here is Gloria at her first Newport Coaching event in 2006.

COACHES AND COACHING THROUGHOUT THE AGES

In 2000, Gloria participated with the coach and four at the Devon Horse Show. She is wearing a brimless hat since the class was held in the evening

Gloria is driving a four-in-hand of Kladruber Horses from the Czech Republic to an English style road coach, accompanied by Equine Specialist, Kacy Tipton, Horn Sounder, Dale Romagnoli, and groom Michelle Dlugborski. All road coaches had names and this one is named the Sir Walter Scott after the romantic writer of England.

Queen's Golden Jubilee, UK

Gloria drove four of her young three-year-old Friesian Horses at the Queen's Golden Jubilee Celebration in 2002. Robert Jennings won an award for this photograph. Gloria is with Coachman, David Saunders, Horn Sounder, Dale Romagnoli and Groom, Sharon Romagnoli. Melissa Wariner is standing at the wheelers. The Road Coach requires a special utilitarian harness with brown or tan collars and "hit and miss" brow bands on the horses' heads. Grooms are in less formal livery and the Guard who sounds the horn is in a brightly colored uniform.

Contributing to this book is Gloria's personal coachman, David E. Saunders, who has worked with horses all of his adult life. His insights have helped Gloria and contributed to this book. He is pictured driving the Austin Grays at Disney World, Orlando, Florida to Cinderella's pumpkin carriage. He is also shown driving at SECAB, a breed show in Seville, Spain for purebred Spanish horses. He is presenting the unique "Gloria's Diamond" - one horse in the wheel position, two horses in the swing position and one horse in the lead.

Disney World, Orlando, Florida

SECAB, Seville, Spain

COACHES AND COACHING THROUGHOUT THE AGES

Gloria in Munster, Germany

Gloria at Newport, 2015

Gloria participated in the World Coaching Club Meet at the Kentucky Horse Park in Lexington, Kentucky. She is accompanied by Coachman David E. Saunders, Danielle and Henk Van der Weil of Belgium, and Horn Sounder Ray Tuckwiller of West Virginia. Gray horses that turn white with age, have been valued throughout history.

Gloria driving at Windsor Castle for the Queen's 90th birthday.

"TWIG, TWEET, AND TROT"
A coaching tune,
dedicated to Gloria Austin
by The Canadian Tootlers, 1998

APPENDIX

Terms

A long set - Two cockhorses.
Artist - A great coachman.
Benjamin - A greatcoat worn by a coachman
Both sides of the road - a team worked up and back a stage, the same day (sometimes called two sweats.)
Boot - Projections at the side or rear of the coach
Chapman - A trader.
Cockhorse - An additional horse to assist the team on steep hills. Ridden by a postillion.
Crab – the end of the pole
Cross team - Two grays and two darker horses.
"Feather edging it" - Driving very close to another carriage.
Gamon seat - The second seat on a coach. A back gamon is the rear-facing seat on coach roof.
Hackney man - a man who rented horses.
Handling the ribbons - The manipulation of the reins.
Jobmaster - The person that hired out horses, harness and vehicles and either carried on business at a coach office or at an inn.
Leaders - Front pair of four or six horses
Light horse - The gray or horse with white markings driven as a lead horse to be seen at night.
Mail Coach - called "The Mail"
Mail Receiving Office - The country inn which received letters.
"Putting to" - harnessing and hitching the horses
"Springing the team" - to put the horses in a canter at the bottom of a steep hill.
Stagecoach - Public coach running over an advertised route with names like Rocket and Telegraph
Stage - The distance between one change of horse and another.
Swing - Middle pair of six horses
Wheelers - Rear pair of four or six horses.

Time-Line And Trivia

- Roman rider delivered messages by horseback all over the Roman Empire.
- In the ninth century, riders of Germany, France, and Italy had established route for delivering the post by horseback over most of Europe.
- 1300 AD- Flanders Carriage - no springs and no turntable
- 1400-1500 AD - horse litter Muletaire
- 1400-First official Post (delivery by carriage with change of horses) was formed under the rule of Roger I of Germany. Leonard of Thurn and Taxis was named Postmaster General of the Charles V's Empire.
- 1516-The Post was established in Brussels and Vienna
- 1555-First carriages in England -called coaches
- 1580-Earl of Arundel of France brought a coach to Queen Elizabeth I of England Most traveled on foot or horseback but ladies often traveled in coaches.
- The Swiss Diligence was the predecessor of the English coach.
- 1564-The Stage Wagon (or stagecoach) came into use. It was roomy with broad wheels.
- 1605-Hackney coaches (coaches for hire) were used in and around the streets of London
- 1625-A patent was granted to Edward Knapp for "hanging the bodies of the carriages on springs of steel. Not effective until 40 years.
- 1636-6,000 coaches (carriages), private and hackney, were used in London. Sedan chairs were for hire.
- 1640-Stage coaches came into vogue in England.
- 1650-Glass windows were used in coaches.
- 1662-2,490 hackney (for hire) coaches (carriages) were in use in London. Laws were instituted to improve roads and 400 of these public carriages were licensed. There were only six stagecoaches in use at this time and they worked short stages of 20-40 miles, changing horses in route.
- 1670-Springs were in general use 17th Century roads were terrible so there was great effort put into improving the carriage. Carriages were scorned because they rutted the dirt streets of London.
- 1694-Taxing of hackney (for hire) cabs brought in great revenue and helped to finance the war with France. 700 cabs were taxed and even so cab driving and renting chairs were lucrative occupation.
- In 1703 when the weather was good, the coach from London to Portsmouth did the journey of about ninety miles, in fourteen hours.

COACHES AND COACHING THROUGHOUT THE AGES

- 1706-The York coach left London on Monday, Wednesday and Friday. Performing the 200-mile journey in four days; each passenger was allowed 14 pounds of luggage.
- In the 18th century, one could travel forty miles per day and there was no nighttime travel because of the audacity of highwaymen.
- "The Machine" of the late 1600s - the driver's seat was not suspended. The application of springs to stagecoaches allowed for the carrying of passengers on the roof of the coach.
- 1737-Benjamin Franklin was named the first Postmaster General for the American colonies.
- In 1775, stagecoaches generally carried eight persons inside and often 10 outside passengers. There were upwards of 400 stagecoaches, flies, machines and diligences and over 17,000 wheeled carriages.
- Diligences were called "long coaches" and suspended on what were called heavies, carried six passengers on the inside and twelve on the out.
- 1780-The postal service was bad; the coach covered the distance from Bath to London in 16 to 18 hours and the post boys on horseback traveled along and took 40 hours to cover the same distance.
- John Palmer who managed the Theaters Royal of Bath and Bristol, proposed a special coach carrying the mail with a guard (ex-soldiers) be instituted to protect the mail and travel at a speed of eight miles per hour. It was very punctual.
- On August 2, 1784, the first mail coach left the Rummer Tavern at 4 o'clock and arrived in London at the Swan with Two Necks well before eight o'clock the following morning.
- In 1815, Instructions to the Guard were "not to quit or desert the Mail or suffer any loitering or stopping at public houses." Guards were dismissed, suspended or fined if failed to deliver letter bags. The Snow Book, as it was called, was the guards log of incidents occurring in route. As the name suggests the incident might be a snowstorm disabling the coach. In this event, it was the guard's responsibility to take two horses from the hitch, ride one and place the mail on the other and continue on his way.
- Passenger fares on a Mail Coach
    4d. to 5d. per mile for outsiders
    8d. to 10d. per mile for insiders
- Passenger fares on an ordinary stagecoach
    2 Yd. to 3d. per mile for outsiders
    4d. to 5d. per mile for insides

- A seat on a Mail Coach was highly desirable since the mail was not to be delayed. It did not have to stop and the turnpike toll stations and was mandated to be on time. One is said to be able to set his clock by the passing of the mail coach.
- 1818- John Macadam ushered in the 'golden age of coaching' by developing a revolutionary system of building roads with crushed stone 6 oz of weight. A one-foot layer of the crushed stone, stamped and rolled, was to provide the horse and carriage the necessary platform on which to give the passenger speed and comfort. Mail delivery could now be quickened.
- The Quicksilver mail coach did 216 miles in 21 hours and 14 minutes, including stoppages.
- Driving for pleasure came about in the 17th century with improvements in roads. George IV and others took full advantage with the use of private carriages and driving for pleasure.
- In France roads were to be 4 degrees and 46". 7 to 8 degrees was maximum for horses and carriage.
- The Landau invented at Landau in Germany in 1757 and in 1790 made to open in the middle of the roof of 'hood' was a popular carriage combining the advantages of a closed and open carriage.
- In 1819, it is reported that there were upwards of 70 coaches traveling to and from Brighton's seaside resorts and London each day.
- In 1835, there were 700 mail coaches and just fewer than 3,300 stages running in England. 150,000 horses were used while 30,000 men were employed as coachman, guards, horse keepers and hostlers. Mr. W. Chaplin was the largest proprietor. He had five "yards" in London and owned 1,300 horses.

SOURCES

HISTORY OF COACHES and COACHING
https://archive.org/stream/carriagescoaches00stra/carriagescoaches00stra_djvu.txt
https://archive.org/details/coachingage00sturgoog/page/n26
http://www.searchengine.org.uk/dailyebook/Stage-coach%20and%20mail%20in%20days%20of%20yore%20-%20a%20picturesque%20history%20of%20the%20coaching%20age%20(1903)%20Volume%202.pdf

HISTORY OF TRANSPORTATION IN THE BRITISH ERAS
http://www.localhistories.org/transport.html
http://victorian-era.org/victorian-times-transport.html
https://horsesandhistory.wordpress.com/2011/05/02/transport-and-carriages-in-the-victorian-era-1837-1901/
http://twoworlds-history.blogspot.com/p/victorian-and-edwardian-whats.html
http://driehausmuseum.org/blog/view/the-manners-of-the-edwardian-era
http://jessicaleake.com/riding-during-the-edwardian-era/
Edwardian England: A Guide to Everyday Life, 1900-1914 By Evangeline Holland

CONSTRUCTION
American Horse-Drawn Vehicles. Written by Jack D. Rittenhouse
History of New Haven County, Connecticut, Volume 1 edited by John L. Rockey
https://en.wikipedia.org/wiki/Obadiah_Elliott
Annals of the Road: Notes on Mail and Stage Coaching in Great Britain, by Captain Malet, 1876
https://archive.org/details/annalsofroadorno00male/page/n23
https://www.thevintagenews.com/2016/09/01/priority-charvolants-extremely-elegant-kite-drawn-carriages/

TYPES: STAGECOACHES/MAIL COACHES/PARK DRAG/GALA/FRENCH
English Wayfaring Life in the Middle Ages by Jusserand
https://www.lutonculture.com/stockwood-discovery-centre/gardens-and-galleries/mossman/
https://en.wikipedia.org/wiki/Claude_Duval#Highwayman
Old and New Edinburgh, Volume V, Page 152

https://www.historic-uk.com/CultureUK/The-Stagecoach/

Carriages & Coaches : Their History and Evolution By Ralph Straus https://archive.org/stream/carriagescoaches00stra/carriagescoaches00stra_djvu.txt

The Coaching Age by Stanley Harris, 1896-https://archive.org/details/coachingage00sturgoog/page/n26

Stage-coach and mail in days of yore : a picturesque history of the coaching age by Charles G. Harper http://www.searchengine.org.uk/dailyebook/Stage-coach%20and%20mail%20in%20days%20of%20yore%20-%20a%20picturesque%20history%20of%20the%20coaching%20age%20(1903)%20Volume%202.pdf

Annals of the Road: Mail and Stagecoaching in Great Britain by Captain Malet 1876 https://archive.org/details/annalsofroadorno00male/page/n11

The English Mail-coach by Thomas De Quincey https://ebooks.adelaide.edu.au/d/de_quincey/thomas/english-mail-coach/chapter1.html

https://englishhistoryauthors.blogspot.com/2016/12/coaching-inns-in-early-19th-century.html

https://www.wikiwand.com/en/Stage_station

https://www.thoughtco.com/john-loudon-mcadam-1991690

The Carriage Journal: Vol 55 No 2 March 2017

AMERICA GETS ITS COACHES

The Golden Age: 1860–1932." Boundless Political Science. Boundless, 21 Jul. 2015. Retrieved 25 Dec. 2015

http://daytoninmanhattan.blogspot.com/2015/03/the-lost-webb-and-twombly-houses-nos.html

https://theberkshireedge.com/connections-coaching-and-driving-in-the-gilded-age/

http://thegildedageera.blogspot.com/2012/07/mrs-charles-b-alexander-mansion-new.html

HORSES

HISTORICAL SOCIETY OF OLD YARMOUTH STAGECOACH DAYS by Pat Tafra

https://www.horsenation.com/2012/04/02/horses-in-history-britains-royal-mews/

https://en.wikipedia.org/wiki/Coach_(carriage)#Coach_horses

http://home.claranet.nl/users/lijssel/nederlnd/The%20Origins%20of%20the%20Warmblood%20Horse.htm

DRIVING
Manual of Coaching by Fairman Rogers. Published by J.B. Lippincott Company London, 1901
Hints on Driving by Captain C. Morley Knight
Von Achenbach, B. Hitching and Driving. Verlag Dr. Rudolf Georgi, Aachen, Germany, 1922
Wheels by Edwin Tunis, 1955

BOOKS
On the Box Seat by Tom Ryder
The Coaching Era by Violet A. Wilson
The Coaching Age aby Stanley Harris; Richard Bentley & Son, London, 1885
Old Coaching Days by Stanley Harris; Richard Bentley & Son, London, 1882
Driving by Clive Richardson
Stage-coach and Mail in Days of Yore by Charles George Harper, 1903
A Manuel of Coaching by Fairman Rogers;
Driving by Francis M. Ware; Doubleday, Page & Company, 1903
The Private Stable by James A. Garland; Little, Brown, and Company, 1902
Hints on Driving by Captain C. Morley Knight; J. A. Allen & Co. LTD., 1884
Driving Lessons by E. Howlett; Byram-Cum-Sutton, 1992
The History of Coaches by G. A. Thrupp; Kerby & Endean, London, 1877
Coaching Roads of Old New England by George Francis Marlowe; The Macmillan Company, New York, 1945
Historic UK, The Stagecoach by Ben Johnson

www.ingramcontent.com/pod-product-compliance
Lightning Source LLC
Chambersburg PA
CBHW061126070526
44584CB00033B/4236